SURVIVING THE STORMS

SURVIVING THE STORMS

EXTRAORDINARY STORIES OF COURAGE AND COMPASSION AT SEA

Lifeboats

with Nikki Girvan

HarperCollins*Publishers*

HarperCollins*Publishers*
1 London Bridge Street
London SE1 9GF

www.harpercollins.co.uk

HarperCollins*Publishers*
1st Floor, Watermarque Building, Ringsend Road
Dublin 4, Ireland

First published by HarperCollins*Publishers* 2020
This edition published 2021

1 3 5 7 9 10 8 6 4 2

Text © RNLI 2020

Nikki Girvan asserts the moral right to
be identified as the author of this work

RNLI name and logo are trademarks of RNLI
used by HarperCollins*Publishers* Limited
under licence from RNLI (Sales) Ltd

A catalogue record of this book is
available from the British Library

ISBN 978-0-00-839540-7

Printed and bound in Great Britain by
CPI Group (UK) Ltd, Croydon

MIX
Paper from
responsible sources
FSC™ C007454

This book is produced from independently certified FSC™ paper
to ensure responsible forest management.

For more information visit: www.harpercollins.co.uk/green

This book is dedicated to all the lifesavers and their families around the UK and Ireland.

We are one crew.

CONTENTS

FOREWORD

by HRH The Duke of Kent

In the fifty years that I have had the honour of serving as President of the Royal National Lifeboat Institution, it has been a pleasure to meet hundreds of courageous volunteers all around the coasts of the UK and Ireland. I can tell you that no two lifeboat crews are the same; they are each made up of volunteers from many different backgrounds, launching from stations with their own unique histories and coastal challenges.

Yet there is something that binds every RNLI lifesaver. They show a special sort of kindness that compels them to answer calls for help from strangers. That is the spirit that led to the formation of the Institution nearly 200 years ago. The charity looks very different in the twenty-first century, with its sophisticated craft, and the development of newer ways of saving lives through lifeguarding and education work. Many things have stayed the same, though – the selfless spirit still runs true.

I was, therefore, delighted to hear that a book would be produced that celebrates RNLI rescues from the twenty-first century, recounting remarkable rescues in the lifesavers' own words. In these pages you will read dramatic – yet typically modest – accounts from brave and skilful people. Many of them were recognised with special awards for their actions, and it was a privilege to present Medals for Gallantry to some of these lifesavers personally.

We owe a great debt of gratitude to all the crew members, lifeguards and survivors whose true stories appear in this book. It will raise crucial funds to help the charity save more lives at sea.

I hope you enjoy reading every page as much as I did. I also hope you share my utmost admiration for the remarkable people of the RNLI, who volunteer to save lives around our coastlines every single day. Thank you so much for your support.

INTRODUCTION

by Mark Dowie, Chief Executive of the RNLI

Have our nations ever owed more to those who put themselves in harm's way to help others in a crisis? In recent times, we have seen how the best of people are prepared to combine their skills, courage and kindness to ensure that we can survive the storm. For the RNLI's life-saving communities, that sort of sacrifice has been a way of life since 1824.

Prior to joining the RNLI as Chief Executive in May 2019, I was privileged to serve alongside the volunteer crew at Salcombe Lifeboat Station. It was my responsibility to make the call on whether to deploy a lifeboat, sometimes in the most extreme conditions, requiring careful judgement in balancing the safety of the crew and saving lives at sea.

Having seen their selfless courage and commitment first-hand, they deserve recognition, even though it's the last thing on their mind when they answer the call for help. Each lifeboat crew member and lifeguard who features in this book has their own unique, fascinating story. As well as recalling the drama involved in saving others at sea, they also share their motivations and emotional stories from their own lives.

There is, of course, no book big enough to do justice to every RNLI rescue and rescuer. There are hundreds of lifeboat stations, and thousands of crew members and lifeguards. Between them, they have helped so many people survive the storms. I would therefore like to take this opportunity to send my sincere thanks to Every One who has played a part in saving lives at sea over nearly 200 years of the RNLI's history. As the owner of this book, that now includes you too.

This is Our Watch for the RNLI. Like generations of life-savers before us, it's our job to keep this special charity safe and secure for the next 200 years, so it can continue to save lives while being loved and treasured by so many.

Thank you for buying this book, and for supporting the RNLI. May it bring you hope and warmth after stormy times.

A LEAP OF FAITH

Mark Criddle, Torbay 2008

The wind was howling and the rain was lashing RNLI Torbay Lifeboat Station as I looked at my watch.

Almost seven o'clock.

I put down my cup of tea, turned my gaze away from the darts on the television and looked out of the window. It had been wild outside all day. Screaming gales were tearing through the usually calm horseshoe bay, whipping the waves up high; frothy and white, even before they crashed against the shore. Yet despite this, the radio in the station had been quiet and I couldn't see anything on the horizon. So, I allowed my mind to wander onto more domestic matters.

I wonder if that drying is finished yet?

Since my children, Marsden, four and Maitland, seven, had arrived, my wife Melanie and I were constantly overwhelmed by the amount of washing that two small boys managed to create. In the winter months, I forever found myself drying piles of wet clothes in Brixham Marina's launderette, next door to the lifeboat station. Grabbing my pager and zipping up my jacket, I battled against the wind back to the launderette and reached into the dryer I'd filled twenty minutes earlier.

Still wet! I tutted.

Pushing the door firmly shut, I turned to sit on a bench opposite the dryers, but before my bottom had time to hit the seat, my pager jolted to life. It was Ken James, the deputy launching authority for Torbay, calling for an immediate launch. As coxswain for the station, I swung into action.

Abandoning my washing, I darted straight back to the boathouse and got on the telephone to find out what Ken knew about the incident.

'There's a coaster about 34 miles south-east of Berry Head,' he said. 'She's listing, and the captain called the coastguard for assistance.'

'How many crew on board?' I asked.

'Twenty in total, we think,' he said.

Berry Head was a coastal headland and the southern boundary of Tor Bay in Devon. The *Ice Prince*, a 6,395-gross-tonne Greek-registered vessel, was carrying timber down the English Channel from Sweden through to Egypt. She'd been caught by the gale-force winds and strong waves, and was now tilting on her side, her cargo shifting the more she leaned.

So far, so straightforward, I thought.

As dramatic as it sounded, it wasn't particularly uncommon. In fact, the previous coxswain, David Hurford, and I had escorted the vessel's sister ship into Brixham a few years earlier.

I wasn't overly concerned. The weather was going to make things hairy, and it was going to be a bigger incident than usual. But it was still just an escort job.

Since I'd been next door in the marina, I was the first to reach the station, but I wasn't on my own for long. Within minutes, bodies began to burst into the station from all over town. Before I knew it, there were thirteen volunteers at the station, all ready and raring to go – the fact that the weather was so wild was getting them even more excited than usual. They knew that any job in these conditions would be a challenge, and challenges were what we trained for.

We'd been asked to launch our Severn class lifeboat, the *Alec and Christina Dykes*, and stand by at the scene, with a less powerful Tyne class lifeboat from RNLI Salcombe following behind us. I looked round at the thirteen assembled crew members, faces excited and expectant, and sighed inwardly.

I hated this part.

Only seven of us could go out.

I was coxswain and it was my job to choose.

As a full-time mechanic with twenty years in the RNLI, I'd often joked about being made coxswain, but I never really expected it to happen. When David retired and I was asked to step into his shoes, I couldn't believe my luck.

Even two years on, I had to pinch myself occasionally. I loved having responsibility for my crew, my lifeboat and the people we were sent to help.

But I never enjoyed picking who to take out.

Every single one of those volunteers had dropped everything to get down to the station and get on our boat. They'd left jobs, partners and children without a second thought. They were all willing to risk their own lives to help others. Just like myself, when I'd started volunteering, they all *wanted* to go out. In my eyes, they all *deserved* to go out.

But with thirteen people and only six spaces, I was going to have to disappoint someone.

It was a feeling I remembered all too well.

I'd known from a young age what the lifeboats meant to their crew.

Back then, when you heard the maroons go off – two loud rockets that would be shot out towards sea – you knew exactly what was happening.

A lifeboat was being launched!

Pagers were rarer than hen's teeth in those days. There was one for the launching authority, one for the mechanic and one for the coxswain. Everyone else had to keep their ears peeled for the maroons.

If they went off while I was at my nán and grandad's house, I had front-row seats. They lived on a hairpin bend facing the shipyard, just a hundred metres or so from the lifeboat station.

We were so close you'd feel the vibration in your bones. Then, moments later, cars would come screaming round that hairpin bend, as crew members raced to the station. If there was a shout, they all wanted to be part of it.

You see, our coastal community was built around fishing, shipping and seaside tourism. Most of us had spent our childhoods out on boats or in the water. The lifeboat was our town's safeguard. The volunteers were local teachers, parents, plumbers and much more. But when those maroons went off, they were RNLI crew, above everything else.

I was fascinated. Sometimes I'd even run down to the shipyard and onto the front, just to watch the lifeboat powering out to sea.

What would it be like to be part of that? I'd wonder.

Eventually, at the age of 19, I plucked up the courage to ask the coxswain, Arthur Curnow, if I could join the crew. Coxswains were renowned for being tough and fearsome, so it had taken me two years to build up the nerve. I can't even remember what I said to Arthur that day. But I remember his response.

'What are you doing tomorrow?' he asked.

'Nothing,' I said, puzzled.

Surely it wasn't going to be that easy?

'Bring a chipping hammer down to my tugboat,' he said. 'I have a job for you.'

'OK,' I nodded.

As well as being the coxswain, Arthur had some boats himself and employed a few people from around town to work on them.

The next day, Arthur still hadn't answered my question, but I found myself chipping rust off his tugboat nonetheless. In fact, it happened again and again and again.

Why am I here doing this for no money? I thought one day.

But deep down, I knew why. As well as a bit of free labour for Arthur, this was also a test. *Would I turn up tomorrow with that chipping hammer? Was I prepared to go and do something, no questions asked? Would I do a good job, even without pay?*

If I did, he knew I'd make good crew. So I did what he asked.

It took almost a year to get my answer, when Arthur invited me out on a training exercise one day. The crew were doing man-overboard drills on a miserable, blustery day, when he called over to me.

'Come on, then,' he said, beckoning me to the wheelhouse of the *Edward Bridges*, an old wooden Arun class lifeboat. 'Come up and have a go.'

I couldn't believe it. Sucking in a deep breath, I took the wheel with as much confidence as I could muster.

I'm driving a bloody lifeboat. What's that about? I thought, grinning from ear to ear as I crashed through the waves.

I couldn't contain my excitement when I got home.

'Arthur let me drive the boat today!' I exclaimed, bursting through the door and regaling my mum and dad with every single detail.

Just like that, I was crew.

And just like that, I was hooked.

But it didn't mean I got to see much action. Not for a long while. Back then there was a crew of more than thirty and roughly eighteen shouts a year. I didn't often get picked, but I made it my business to always turn up.

Just like my crew had tonight.

Plenty had changed since I'd first volunteered in 1988. For one, Arthur's little initiation ploy was a thing of folklore now, something we all laughed about. Recruitment was a stricter process these days. The maroons had gone as well, with all crew now having their own pagers. And although we were regularly doing over one hundred shouts a year, it could still be just as tough to get picked.

But there were some things that never changed. The commitment of the crew. The camaraderie. That desire to go out in any conditions. That willingness to always show up – even if you might not be picked.

That was exactly what I could see in the thirteen brave crew members who'd turned up tonight. The anticipation in their faces snapping me back to the task at hand. Obviously, I would be going. My crew were my responsibility. But now we were ready to launch and – whether I liked it or not – I had to pick my crew for tonight's job.

Who would be most appropriate?

Looking round the room, I made my selection.

'Roger Good,' I said, indicating the crew's second coxswain.

'Mat Tyler.' He was our station mechanic and full-time crew like me.

'Alex Rowe and John Ashford.' Alex was a doctor and John a paramedic. Their professional skills were always useful to have on board. Then finally I called out the last two names.

'Nigel Coulton and Darryll Farley.'

Without further discussion, we kitted up, ran out to our lifeboat, the *Alec and Christina Dykes*, and, at 7.44pm, we sped out of the station.

Almost immediately the wild conditions were evident. Driving at fifteen knots, we found ourselves crashing against the waves.

'We're going to have to strap in,' I shouted, as I steered the boat in the direction of the stricken ship. 'It's going to get pretty nasty.'

It was something we almost never had to do, but tonight it was essential. We had a two-hour journey ahead of us. I couldn't have my crew getting injured on our way if we caught a bad wave.

It was going to be a long night.

We were making progress towards our destination, when – fifteen minutes into our journey – the radio crackled to life. It was a call from the captain of the *Ice Prince*. His tone made my ears prick up immediately.

'There's water in the engine,' he said. 'The engine has stopped.'

I frowned as the words sank in. The rising panic in his voice was evident.

But you were just listing a minute ago, I thought.

'The engine has stopped?' I repeated, to confirm I'd heard correctly.

'Yes,' came the reply. 'I'm drifting.'

'OK,' I said. 'Understood.'

This changed everything.

The urgency escalated immediately. With no engine, there was no control. The ship was even more vulnerable to the sea's swell and the howling winds now.

We had to take it up a notch.

I turned to my helm, Roger.

'Increase our speed to twenty knots,' I said. Roger reacted immediately. It would knock around twenty minutes off our journey time. As Roger powered us on, my brain ticked over.

What were we going to find at the scene?

I'd expected a routine escort job, but now I knew I had to be prepared for more. The coastguard helicopter *India Juliet* had even been tasked with evacuating some of the ship's crew. As we got closer, the situation seemed to be deteriorating by the minute.

Yet another update crackled out of the radio.

'One of my crew was washed against the *sshhhhh shhhh*,' came the voice of the captain. 'He's *sssshhhh*.'

I struggled to understand the message over the cabin noise and radio interference, but I could *feel* the fear in his voice.

'Can you repeat that?' I said.

'He's *shhhh* broken *shhhh* leg …'

I didn't know exactly what had happened, but there was an injury. If there had been one, there could be more.

After that, we went full throttle. Roger really opened the lifeboat up and charged out, about fifteen miles east of Berry Head. Finally, the *Ice Prince* came into view.

I stepped out of the shelter of the wheelhouse and moved up to the flying bridge to evaluate the scene. My eyes adjusted to the darkness and I could see the outline of the ship looming. Then my jaw hit the floor – it was like nothing I'd witnessed before in my career.

She was groaning as she leaned at more than forty degrees, rails touching the surface of the waves, battered by winds that were reaching up to fifty miles per hour.

'How is this thing still afloat?' I gasped.

Looking at my crew, I knew they were thinking the same. We could hear *India Juliet*'s rotor blades whirring above us and saw a thin beam from her lights intertwined with lights from HMS *Cumberland*, a Royal Navy frigate that was standing by on station, illuminating the unfolding drama.

The crew of the *Ice Prince* were gathering in the ship's wheelhouse, before struggling over to the ship's bridge wing, where *India Juliet*'s winchman was battling against the elements to winch them up, using a hi-line to try to control their movement as they were zipped up past the ship's flailing mast and aerials.

It emerged that the plan had been to remove the injured man and eleven of his comrades, while a skeleton of eight senior crew would remain on board to try to start the pumps while we worked with RNLI Salcombe to escort the vessel to safety.

But with no engine, and news coming over the radio that its generator had gone down as well, she was what we called a 'dead ship' – a vessel that could no longer move under its own power.

What's more, she was beam on to the weather. The worst possible position she could be in.

One side of the ship calm, the other rough, and everything conspiring to capsize her.

'A decent set of waves is going to come through at any minute,' I said to Roger. 'She's going to roll over.'

'There's no way this thing's going to stay afloat,' he agreed. 'And there's still crew on there.'

We both knew that this could very easily turn into a rescue job. And a serious one at that. While *India Juliet* was continuing to try to take her casualties, I powered the lifeboat around the ship.

If I had to get people off, how would I do it?

Our lifeboat was much smaller than the *Ice Prince*, so I needed to find safe access points that were a similar height to our lifeboat. Two decades' worth of shouts flew through my head. I called up all the knowledge I had and all the conversations I'd had with coxswains who'd seen big jobs like this one. I considered every option.

Get up alongside the ship, get your crew into a life raft and rescue them to the raft …

I shook my head. A life raft would be tossed around like paper in those waves and my crew wouldn't be safe. It wasn't an option.

The ship crew wear thermal suits. It's easier to get them in the water, chuck them a line and pull them into the boat …

But there was debris everywhere and the sea's swell was unpredictable. Plus, I didn't fancy our chances of convincing anyone to jump into *that* sea …

Just then, the voice of *India Juliet*'s pilot crackled over the radio. As the weather worsened, it had become harder and harder for the winchman to control the line in the heavy swell and rain squalls, and he'd had to keep cutting the hi-line free to avoid catastrophe. But they'd managed it.

Now they were at capacity.

'We have our twelve casualties,' he announced. 'We're returning to Portland.'

It was good news, but there were still eight people left on the ship. In these conditions, with casualties to drop off and fuel to be topped up, it could be more than an hour before the helicopter returned.

As it turned and headed back in the direction of the coast, rotor blades slicing through the gale-force winds and rain, I radioed the skipper of the *Ice Prince*.

'What's your intention, captain?' I asked. I knew what the answer *should* be, but it wasn't my call. The ship's captain had to make the decision.

Wait for the helicopter or abandon ship now.

'My intention is to abandon ship to you,' he said without hesitation. 'I need to get us off this ship right away.'

I didn't blame him. I certainly wouldn't have chosen to stay on board. The list was now so great that the ship's rails were partially submerged under the water.

It would only take one strong set of waves and …

I shook the thought from my head. With the captain's intentions confirmed, it was our turn. Now *I* had to make my decision.

How the hell were we going to do this?

Getting the ship's crew in the water might have worked in other conditions, on other rescues. But I knew the casualties would be tired and scared. We'd have a job convincing them to jump into a heaving sea, gale howling, and telling them it would all be fine.

There had to be another way.

During my recce, I had come up with a plan. It wouldn't be easy, but I believed it would work. I returned to the wheelhouse and called Roger.

'Right, Rog. This is what we're going to do,' I said. 'We'll tell the captain to gather his crew at the stern of the ship, near the winch for the stern anchor. That's about the same height as our bow.'

'OK,' Roger nodded, noting every detail.

'I'll drive up to the ship, keep the bow into the weather,' I continued. 'If they climb over the rail, we should be able to get them from there.'

We decided we'd have five men on our bow to help pull the crew over – Roger, Nigel, Alex, John and Mat. Darryll would stay with me on the flying bridge to assist with steering and to control our searchlight, the only adequate source of light we had to cut through the pitch darkness. When we got close enough to the stern of the *Ice Prince*, our five crew members would be able to grab each survivor and pull them over to our foredeck.

'If anyone goes in the water,' I said to Roger, 'we will have RNLI Salcombe standing by to assist.'

'Right, I've got it,' said Roger.

'Don't take anybody off until I'm ready,' I said. 'And make sure it's safe.'

Roger knew the score, but the job was already dangerous enough. I didn't want anyone taking unnecessary risks.

As he led our team to the foredeck, I confirmed our plan with RNLI Salcombe. Then I radioed the *Ice Prince* captain and explained my plan step-by-step. I knew once they left the wheelhouse, our communication would be limited, especially since many of the ship's crew didn't speak English. We'd have to rely on hand signals and shouting over a roaring gale to get the job done.

Fortunately, he was on board with what I proposed.

'We'll make our way out now,' the captain confirmed.

And that was it.

So we had all agreed to the plan. We just had to stick to it.

I climbed out into the thrashing wind and rain, and up to the flying bridge. With no intercom, all *I* could do was rely on the captain and his crew doing what we'd agreed, and my crew doing what we'd agreed.

It was easy to feel crushed by pressure. But over the years I'd learned to keep a cool head. As the radio fell silent, my mind went quiet too.

No more discussion. Just get it done.

I knew that was how successful rescues worked. I settled on my one single focus. Keeping crew, casualties and our boat safe.

Bringing them all home.

Blood pulsed in my ears as we made our test approaches, gauging how best to go alongside the ship and ascertaining what gave us the best position to pull the casualties over.

After a few attempts, I looked over at Roger and the crew positioned on the foredeck and gave a thumbs-up, which was promptly returned.

We were ready.

The adrenaline coursing through my body spiked as they shouted for the first man to scramble over the two anchor winches, a flagpole and across a deck that was now tilted at forty-five degrees to the rail we planned to rescue them from. As he climbed over, my heart was in my mouth. I fought to hold our position and hoped beyond hope that he would grab the split-second window and jump into the arms of my crew.

As I moved alongside the ship, I sucked a deep breath in and watched as he released his grip.

Five sets of arms, all clad in the bright yellow uniform of the RNLI, reached out to grab him. Five brave volunteers, harnessed to a boat in the most appalling sea conditions, all extending their arms to grab a complete stranger and pull him to safety.

Talk about a leap of faith …

Thankfully, we succeeded.

In a heartbeat, the man was on our foredeck, shaken but safe.

If I'd had time to think, I'd have been overwhelmed with pride.

But there was still a lot of work to do.

One down. Seven to go.

With Darryll expertly illuminating my path, I manoeuvred the lifeboat away and prepared for a second approach, then a third. Both times we managed to stay a safe distance apart from the ship.

Both times the crew members landed safely. As Nigel ushered them down below, there were cuts and bruises, but no major injuries.

I took a long, slow breath.

Things are going well.

Or at least, they were. As we went in for our fourth approach, I knew immediately that something was wrong. Instead of jumping, the man stayed glued to the spot. Through the rain and sea spray, even I could see that he was terrified.

We came around again and again, but he couldn't make the jump.

'We're going to have to get closer!' shouted Roger. 'So we can grab him and pull him over.'

'OK,' I yelled.

Darryll and I worked together on the approach, trying to get as close as possible without touching the ship. Each time it wasn't quite enough.

'We need to be closer,' Roger shouted through the darkness.

This is risky, I thought, as I manoeuvred to make another approach. *If we get too close and make contact …*

Suddenly, my worst fear was realised as we caught a bad swell on the starboard side.

CLANG!

There was a massive jolt, and the lifeboat slammed into the side of the *Ice Prince*. The deafening sound of metal against metal tore through the wind and rain, piercing our eardrums. Alex and Mat were sprawled across the foredeck, while the others had just about managed to cling on. Next to me, Darryll had been hit by the searchlight and his head was bleeding.

'Everyone OK?' I shouted.

'All OK here!' came a few shouts from my crew.

True professionals, they just got up and carried on.

We were all right.

Now, what about the ship's crew?

I looked back at the *Ice Prince* and my stomach lurched. The man who'd been clinging onto the rail had vanished from sight. My eyes darted around in the blackness.

Had he fallen? Had we caught him between the boats?

I shuddered.

He'd have been crushed immediately …

All I could do was pull the lifeboat away from the side of the ship. Truth be told, I expected to see a body in the water. But as I peered over, I gasped.

'He's not there!' shouted Alex.

Where had he gone?

Seconds dragged like minutes as we used the searchlight to scan the black expanse around us. Then Mat spotted him.

'He's there. Port side,' he called out. The man had resurfaced in the swell, where the ship was rolling heavily. *And he was moving!*

I allowed myself a moment to heave a sigh of relief. He was OK.

For now.

Once again, our situation had shifted. Now we had a man in the water, with two boats and debris being tossed all over the place.

In line with our plan, I knew that RNLI Salcombe would be preparing to recover the casualty. All we could do was wait.

Stick to the plan.

But then, thankfully and somewhat miraculously, the sea did us a favour. A wave suddenly picked the man up and rolled him back inboard towards the ship. Summoning all the strength he had, he managed to grab onto the ship, clamber back up the tilting deck to the muster point at the stern, before wriggling back into position on the rail.

We tried again to approach and encourage him to jump, but once again he was frozen on the spot.

Could anyone blame him?

The four remaining crew members were shaken to the core as well. No one else was going to be making that jump tonight.

Not after what they'd just seen.

We were going to have to pluck them off ourselves, and there was only one way for us to do that.

'I'm going to have to pin the boats together,' I shouted to Roger. 'You'll have to grab what you can and pull them over.'

It was enormously risky. I'd have to keep contact for as long as I could, to give my crew the best chance, but move away before a wave smashed us into the side of the ship again. We'd been lucky the first time. But who knew what damage another collision might cause?

Then there was the debris to consider. By now a considerable part of the *Ice Prince* was submerged. Massive logs littered the water around us and there were hidden hazards lurking below the surface too.

This was going to get tricky.

But I was single-minded. We had a plan and we were going to stick to it. Heart pounding, I used all the power of the lifeboat to get its shoulder against the ship, to try to stop the movement of the larger vessel.

It didn't work on our first attempt, but we weren't going to give up. Time after time we made our approach as the ship rolled uncontrollably and the rain and wind battered us from all directions. Harnessed tightly to the lifeboat, my crew grabbed and pulled the men over when they could, trying again and again when they missed.

In the end it took an hour and a quarter – and more than fifty approaches – guided only by Darryll and our searchlight.

Finally, we grabbed our last man, the ship's captain.

Yes!

But there was no time for celebration yet. We needed to get our survivors back to land. As Nigel took them down below, it was clear they were all glad to be off the *Ice Prince*. But when we powered back to the lifeboat station, motion sickness began to set in … along with a belated realisation of the severity of the situation they'd found themselves in. They knew they could easily have all been killed.

Just like we could have …

Still pumped full of adrenaline, I wouldn't let my mind go there yet. As coxswain, I was responsible for getting survivors, my crew and my boat back safely.

My job wasn't done yet.

It was quarter past one in the morning when we finally arrived back. Relief and exhaustion began to set in as we helped the survivors off the boat. Two were whisked away in a waiting ambulance, to be treated for shock and minor injuries. For the rest of them, we provided some good old RNLI Torbay hospitality.

'Let's get you one of Ken's famous breakfasts,' I said. As usual, Ken, our deputy launching authority, had prepared a slap-up breakfast of tea and delicious sandwiches.

I sat back and watched as everyone tucked into the food and chatted excitedly about the ordeal.

'I've been on crew for twenty-six years,' Nigel said. 'And this is the best job I've done.' He couldn't contain the pride in his voice. And rightly so.

The crew had been marvellous.

They'd saved eight lives.

In my head, the same moment from the rescue kept playing over and over.

Pulling up towards the ship to see my crew with their arms outstretched, in the pounding rain and gales, risking everything to grab hold of a complete stranger.

It was a moment that I knew would remain with me forever.

What we felt in pride, the *Ice Prince*'s crew felt in gratitude.

'Thank you for saving my life,' said one of the younger guys, smiling broadly, as he sipped his tea. Another guy expressed thanks on behalf of those who couldn't speak English.

'From me and the other crew, one big thanks,' he said.

Sandwiches eaten, rescue reports completed and a few short interviews given to local journalists who'd gotten wind of the shout, I was almost done for the night. I just had one final task to complete before I headed back to Melanie and the kids.

I had to pick up the drying from the launderette.

By the time I got home it was 4.30am. We'd been out for nine and a half hours. As I slipped into our bedroom, Melanie stirred.

'You got called out, didn't you?' she said.

She knew I'd been out, of course. As everything unfolded, Ken had called all the wives and told them to expect a long night.

'Yes, that's right,' I replied.

'All back safe?' she asked.

'Yes.'

'Good.'

Then, after a moment's pause, she continued: 'Did you bring the washing back with you?'

I couldn't help but laugh out loud.

'Yes, all done.' After the night we'd had, I was glad to be home to answer such a mundane question.

The next day I woke, switched on the television and sat in bed trying to muster the energy to get up. I was physically drained, but I knew there was plenty still to do at the station.

More reports, reviewing video footage and checking any damage the lifeboat had sustained.

I knew it had been a big job. But I didn't really realise how big, until my brain, still foggy with sleep, tuned into the news.

'Last night saw a massive rescue in the English Channel,' the reporter announced.

Oh, what's this? I thought, ears pricking up.

'The rescue involved a 6,395-tonne coaster and RNLI lifeboat crews from Torbay and Salcombe,' the reporter continued, over grainy footage of a huge ship listing wildly and a tiny boat bobbing alongside it.

Hang on. That wasn't just any boat.

It was our lifeboat.

Seeing the scale of the incident through black-and-white camera footage from the helicopter, the enormity of what we'd done suddenly dawned on me and my whole body began to shake. It was the most bizarre sensation.

Christ! My head spun. *We did that. That was us!*

I flicked through the channels. The story was everywhere. Timber from the ship had littered the coastline and reporters had been hard at work finding out how it got there.

Melanie must have seen all the fuss too, but she didn't ask about it. We were back safe – and that was all she needed to know. That had always been her way of coping. She knew what I did could be dangerous, but she knew I loved it.

It worked well for our marriage for lifeboat talk to be kept off limits.

I didn't blame her for not wanting to know. I was elated by our success, but as the day went on, the reality of the danger we'd faced started to overwhelm me.

Watching the video footage from different sources, I found my heart pounding. It was no longer just my memory of how it all played out.

It was there in front of me. I could clearly see every risky move and every near miss. My legs and hands began to shake even more violently than they had watching the news report, and emotion bubbled up inside me.

We'd been lucky.

Watching the moment when the boats collided. Watching the crew member plummet into the water. Seeing how small and insignificant we looked being tossed around by the waves. Like David and Goliath.

We'd been really lucky.

Lucky that our lifeboat had withstood the collision. Lucky we'd got everyone off the ship. Lucky that none of our crew had been hurt.

Honestly, I felt sick. Any one of them could have been killed out there, working in those conditions.

And it would have been my fault.

Rewinding and reviewing each minute of footage, I questioned every single one of my decisions over and over. It was a far cry from the clarity and single-mindedness that I'd felt over the course of that night. My responsibility was to my crew, above and beyond everything else.

It was my job to get them home safe to their wives, partners and children.

Had I taken too many chances?

However harshly I criticised myself, though, I knew what the outcome had been. Eight lives were saved and all seven of our crew returned to station – tired, and with a few bruises, but safe. Even our trusty Severn class lifeboat was virtually unscathed. No holes, no serious damage, just a few chunks taken out of the fender. It was remarkable.

A few days later, the crew received a letter from the captain of the HMS *Cumberland*, the frigate that had stood by to assist on the night. It made me beam with pride for my crew.

The letter read: *'It was our great privilege to stand by with ringside seats to watch your determined efforts to take the last eight people off. You handled your lifeboat in extremely challenging conditions. Your actions upheld the finest traditions of the RNLI, earning deserved respect from all involved.'*

As the weeks and months passed, the buzz around the rescue died down. But I slowly started to realise that the *Ice Prince* rescue had been the biggest of my career.

And I'd only been coxswain for a couple of years!

That realisation was cemented when a call came from the RNLI Head Office.

'We'd like to award you the RNLI Silver Medal for Gallantry,' the voice on the phone said. 'For your actions during the *Ice Prince* rescue in January this year.'

Other coxswains had told me that you only ever got one job like this, and here was mine. My career-defining rescue. I was grateful for the award, but it didn't recognise the work of my crew. I felt like everyone on the boat deserved medals as much as I did.

If not more so.

After all, as full-time staff, I'd just done my job. I'd steered the boat, got us out there and made a plan.

The other blokes, all volunteers, they'd done the hard work and put so much more on the line. Eventually, the whole crew went on to win the Pride of Britain Emergency Services Award for our teamwork that night. I was delighted for them.

I was proud to be presented with the RNLI gallantry medal. Especially when I learned that it was the first Silver Medal that had been awarded by the RNLI in three years. But as soon as I got home, I popped it away in a drawer.

It's been there ever since I received it.

I mean no disrespect, but individual accolades just make me uncomfortable. I felt the same way when I received my OBE for services to maritime safety in 2018. By then, I'd served thirty years and been out on more than four hundred shouts. I was honoured and humbled, but I hadn't achieved any of it on my own. I still haven't.

I believe that you're only as good as the people you surround yourself with and I'm extremely lucky to have a supportive family and outstanding crew to serve alongside at Torbay RNLI. I've got three years left now before I retire and I doubt I will ever, ever see another shout like the *Ice Prince*.

Possibly the biggest challenge of my coxswain career came at the very start – and, in many ways, I'm glad. That night pushed me, my crew and the boat to the limits. I think it made me a much wiser leader.

Like other emergency services, no one wants to see an incident like that. Firemen don't *want* to see an out-of-control blaze and RNLI crew don't want to see lives at risk at sea. But it's what we train all of our lives to deal with.

It's our dream job. A test.

Can you do it?

Can you manage?

Can your crew?

You always think you can. You have ultimate trust in your crew. But until you've tested it, how do you know? We all learned a lot about limits that night. I still think about the risks we took. They were huge, but they were the right calls.

I've been told that I'm brave, but if I'm honest, I think the bravest decision any coxswain can make is *not* to have a go. To weigh up if your action can really make a positive difference and then decide that the risk is *too* great.

I was told as a young volunteer, desperate to be picked to go out – *a dead hero is no good to anyone.*

It's a piece of wisdom I continue to share with the crew today.

The *Ice Prince* was an enormous task, but – to this day – I've not had to be brave enough to say no. So perhaps my biggest challenge still lies ahead of me.

2.

PERIL AT SKERRYVORE
David MacLellan, Islay 2016

It was just after midnight on 16 February 2016 when my pager went off. I leapt out of bed and started to get dressed immediately. I didn't even have the chance to look out of my window to check the state of the weather. It was only when I left my house that I realised just how bad the conditions were. As I stepped onto my driveway, I was almost blown off my feet.

Uh-oh …, I thought.

It was dreadful. Blowing a real hooley and with driving rain lashing down angrily. I pulled my coat around me tightly and put my head down as I ran to my car and set off towards the lifeboat station.

Even before I had the full picture, my concern for any casualty vessel and her crew began to mount. This wasn't the kind of weather you'd want to get caught in. I couldn't help but hope that there'd been a mistake.

That it was a false alarm.

But it wasn't. When I arrived at the station five minutes

later, the request for an immediate launch of the lifeboat was still in place.

Down at the station, I saw my dad, Victor MacLellan. He was the deputy launching authority at RNLI Islay Lifeboat Station. As he spoke, I couldn't believe what I was hearing.

'There's a yacht aground on the Skerryvore reef,' he said.

'There's a yacht where?' I asked, to make sure I'd heard correctly.

'Skerryvore,' he said. 'A yacht's run aground on Skerryvore.'

'You've got to be kidding me,' I said. 'There's not a yacht there? At this time of year?'

And at this time of night …

'Apparently there is,' he said.

I was baffled. February wasn't exactly peak yachting season. What's more, Skerryvore was forty miles west of the isle of Islay – a lighthouse sitting on a big rock in the middle of nowhere, with nothing for miles around it.

It just didn't make any sense.

Growing up and living on an island surrounded by other islands, everybody was involved with the sea in some way. Quite often in winter the islands in the Hebrides didn't even have a ferry service, so we were cut off from everything. But you just got on with it.

Islay and neighbouring islands like Barra, up north in the Outer Hebrides, didn't have high-street shops and supermarkets. Many people had crofts, small units of agricultural land with shared hill grazing for sheep and cows, so they could produce lamb and beef. They'd sometimes grow fruit and vegetables or work a tourism aspect into their business too.

But generally crofters always had boats as well. It meant they could go out and catch a few lobsters or crabs to sell on or catch fish for themselves, sometimes salting them and hanging them up to dry out, just to make ends meet.

Although we didn't have a croft, my family were always out on boats, and from primary-school age I'd go out with them. Life on the waves inevitably went hand in hand with an involvement with the RNLI. My dad joined the crew at Islay in 1969, just like many of my family and relatives before and plenty of us afterwards.

Myself included.

I joined the crew at Islay in 1990. In time I married and started a family. For my wife and kids, hearing the pager go off and watching us go out in all conditions was just normal life. My daughters, Katie and Eilidh, would even use the AIS navigation tracking system to see where the boat was heading to when I was out, sometimes staying up late into the night just to watch it. It was all just part of island life, I guess.

Being part of a team and looking after an area where people relied on the sea to make a living, our call outs were often challenging and long, especially in the winter.

To the west of Islay there was an expanse of open water where a lot of big crab boats fished for their produce. After that there was nothing between there and America – you were just exposed to vast and unpredictable open seas. In heavy weather, we'd regularly be called to help large fishing vessels weighing around 160 tonnes, towing them to safety with our forty-five-tonne lifeboat, out for twelve hours at a time.

It was usually summer that brought the yachts. There weren't many marinas or pontoons near Islay, but up north towards Oban and south-east towards the Clyde, they were everywhere.

However, even in good weather conditions it was easy for them to run into problems. Yachts would anchor up in wee bays, the wind would change during the night, their anchors would drag and they'd run aground. When the call for help came, Islay would often be the nearest lifeboat station.

A shout to rescue a yacht that had run aground in the depths of winter, however, was well out of the norm. Especially in a remote and dangerous location like Skerryvore.

It was going to be a rough night.

As full-time coxswain of RNLI Islay's Severn class all-weather lifeboat, I had to pick my crew. We always tried to take seven crew members out on the all-weather lifeboat. That way, if we had to launch the Y-boat, we'd still have five crew on board and two in the smaller boat. In search-and-rescue situations, as well, more eyes on the water were always an advantage.

Tonight, though, five volunteer crew members, including myself, had leapt from their beds and made it to the station within minutes. Our mechanic David McArthur, navigator Thomas Coope and volunteer crew members Duncan McGillivray and Peter Thomson were all kitted up and ready to go.

Seven would have been better, but five would have to do.

'Let's go,' I said.

Time was of the essence, after all.

We all bolted to our lifeboat, the *Helmut Schroder of Dunlossit II*, and climbed on board. Each crew member took up his position. They all knew their role and were completely focused on their individual tasks.

That was what made us such a good team.

Looking at the conditions from the bridge, I knew instantly that navigation was going to be tricky.

'It's going to be a rough one tonight, boys,' I said as we started the engine. 'Get yourselves strapped in.'

In such poor weather, I knew it would be easy to be blown off course, so we'd need to have someone checking our position constantly. I turned to Thomas.

'Don't leave the chart table tonight,' I said.

'OK,' he replied.

'If you see something you're concerned about, let me know,' I added. Thomas nodded in agreement.

As we powered out toward Skerryvore, close to the most westerly island in the Inner Hebrides, Belfast Coastguard confirmed the yacht's estimated position and gave more detail about the shout.

The skipper who'd called for assistance was sailing alone.

I shuddered at the thought. It would be hard enough for a full crew to manage a stricken vessel around that treacherous reef. But a lone skipper?

Almost impossible.

It turned out that RNLI Barra Lifeboat Station had also been alerted to the shout, but they hadn't launched. Skerryvore was smack bang in the middle – about forty miles from them and forty miles from us – but because of the southerly wind behind us, we'd get there quicker.

That's why our pagers had gone off.

The vessel was a fifteen-metre yacht called *Vestavind II*. With her expected position and the appalling weather conditions, we estimated that it would take us about two hours to reach her.

The further out to sea we travelled, the worse the conditions became. Half an hour in we were coming face to face with waves towering between four and six metres in height, accompanied by heavy sleet showers. We had barely got started, and it was already proving to be an extremely challenging service.

And it was about to get even tougher.

While I was at the helm, steering the lifeboat, Thomas called me over the intercom from the chart desk.

'David, we have a problem,' he said.

'What is it?' I asked.

'Our radar has failed,' he said.

A knot tightened in my stomach.

Oh my God …

It was the worst possible time for this to happen, just as we were hitting the really rough weather and heading towards dangerous, rocky shallows.

'Check the breaker,' I said, hoping something had temporarily interrupted it.

'Nothing,' Thomas replied. 'It's gone down.'

Checking the instruments myself, I realised that he was right. Thirty minutes into a shout that I knew could last hours, our radar was completely down.

Pitch black and in the middle of the night, with the wind now reaching a violent storm force 11, we were going to have to rely on Thomas's navigation skills and our own eyes and ears to get us to the yacht.

But it was easier said than done. The lifeboat was being tossed up and down in huge eight-metre swells. Driving rain and spray from the waves meant visibility was poor. As I gripped the helm and battled with the steering, I couldn't see anything apart from an occasional glimpse of the Dubh Artach lighthouse. Between Thomas's chart work and that lighthouse, I fought to keep the boat on course.

Our lack of radar wasn't the only problem we had, either.

'A couple of the crew have taken ill,' said David.

Being stuck in the wheelhouse, bouncing up and down, had left them with their heads in buckets. I knew they'd want to throw open the back door and let the air in, but with waves crashing over the lifeboat and water pouring over the deck, that just wasn't possible.

Water down below could destabilise the whole boat.

We didn't want that happening in these seas.

'OK,' I said. 'Just be extra vigilant until they're over it. Keep the door closed as well.'

That was the thing about being out at sea. You never really knew what was going to happen. You just had to get out there and take what came.

We were down to three pairs of eyes now, so I needed the rest of the crew to have their wits about them even more than usual.

In the conditions that we were experiencing, I wasn't surprised that seasickness had kicked in, but I knew it would pass. The first time it ever happened to me was just before I joined the lifeboat crew. I was working on a fishing boat, and for the first two weeks of my job I suffered seasickness most days.

'You're never going to make it,' the skipper told me.

But I did.

Necessity forced me to work through it, and I knew that the crew would do exactly the same. It wasn't the first time illness had kicked in on a shout. I knew their commitment to getting the job done always pulled them through it quicker.

As we pushed on towards Skerryvore, I concentrated hard, watching the weather, watching the waves and making sure I knew what was coming up ahead. With no radar to guide us, it was more important than ever that we remained vigilant.

As predicted, the seasick crew perked up. By about three o'clock in the morning, as we arrived at the reef, their sickness had passed.

I stopped the boat and, using the lifeboat's searchlight, I scanned the water for the yacht. Without its engine going, our lifeboat felt the full force of the weather, turning head to sea and rolling around wildly.

Up ahead, I could see the lighthouse clearly, but no yacht. Not a trace. My heart sank.

Where was he?

A part of me wasn't surprised. Seeing just how bad the conditions were, feeling our own lifeboat being thrown about by the waves, I knew that if a fifteen-metre yacht had run aground here, the chances of her still being in position were slim. Before we decided what to do next, though, I had to be sure. Could anyone else spot her?

'Are you seeing anything?' I asked the crew.

'Nothing at all,' they all replied.

I shook my head sadly.

He's gone. Skerryvore's claimed him, I thought.

I grabbed my radio and made contact with the coastguard.

'We've arrived at estimated position. The yacht isn't here,' I said.

'Copy that,' the coastguard replied. '*Rescue 100* is searching the area.'

Rescue 100 was Belfast Coastguard's rescue helicopter. While we held position, it undertook a search pattern to see if the yacht could be found nearby. There was every chance that it had been swept further away.

Or capsized completely.

With the crew fearing the worst, the atmosphere on the lifeboat was heavy.

We were too late …

Despite the search effort, we didn't expect good news. Then, suddenly, the radio crackled to life. It was the coastguard.

'We've located the yacht,' he said. '*Rescue 100* is with her at her new position.'

Thank God, I thought.

'Can you confirm the new location?' I asked, as we swung back into action. Thomas scribbled down the new coordinates as the coastguard read them out.

'We'll head out now,' I said.

In the time it had taken for us to reach the original position, the yacht had drifted five miles north and ended up close to the shoal of Outer Hurricane Rock, a turbulent stretch of shallow open water caused by a strong current over the reef.

My stomach lurched. Although the skipper and his yacht were still all right, they were by no means out of danger. Their luck could change at any minute.

We'd also just hit another obstacle. The coastguard informed us that the skipper was Russian.

'He can't speak any English,' the coastguard said. 'We're adding an interpreter into the communications.'

'Understood,' I replied.

But I was concerned. I knew that waiting for our instructions to be translated and then waiting for the skipper's responses to be interpreted for us would add time to everything we did.

Time that we didn't have.

To stand any chance of helping the skipper, we needed to get there, quickly.

Despite learning about the language barrier, we were boosted by the good news that the skipper and his vessel had been found. Guided by *Rescue 100*, we powered towards the new location, rolling over the breaking waves and dipping into their deep troughs as we went.

Before long, the yacht came into sight. She was side on and rolling, being battered by wave after wave that came through. I could also see that the hull had taken a real beating where she'd been dragged over the rocks.

She wasn't in a good way.

As we drew closer I could see the skipper in the wee cockpit at the back of the yacht, wrestling with the boat's steering. He looked absolutely spent.

Like he'd had enough.

It must have been the most uncomfortable night of his life.

The rescue helicopter was struggling too. As the storm raged, it battled against the gale-force winds, bouncing around wildly in the air. It would be too dangerous to attempt an airlift, and she was running out of fuel.

'*Rescue 100* is standing down,' the coastguard communicated. 'It's returning to base to refuel.'

Assessing the stricken vessel's position from the bridge of the lifeboat, my adrenaline levels surged. The yacht was in an incredibly precarious position. To the north I could see the perilous overfalls of Outer Hurricane Rock. The seas were wild around there.

If he were to drift any closer to that …

There'd be nothing we could do. He'd perish.

There was nothing else for it. We had to get a tow attached and pull him away, and we had to do it now.

'We need to get a line over to him,' I said.

The crew immediately readied the tow. If we could convince the skipper to leave his cockpit and grab the line, he'd be able to secure it to the yacht, so we could pull him away from the imminent danger. Battling heavy sleet, the volunteers climbed on deck to the back of the boat and formed a production line, passing the tow along until they were in a position to at least try to pass it over.

Via the radio, our intention was being communicated by the interpreter. But with the sea changing second by second, my crew were using hand signals and shouting to try to explain the plan as well.

'Catch the rope,' shouted David, pointing at the line he was about to throw over. I brought the lifeboat up alongside the yacht and Thomas tried to pass it over, but the skipper didn't come out.

With no one to catch it, the line flopped into the sea. David and the rest of the crew immediately began hauling it in as I came about, ready to make another attempt.

It took about five minutes to come back around, but when we did, we were ready to try again. But the same thing happened.

The skipper still wasn't budging.

Well, who could blame him?

His boat was wallowing about, up and down, up and down. He was probably too scared to move. But he had to. I knew that if we didn't get a line attached, he'd end up being swept away from us.

But every failed attempt made it more difficult for us to get the line across. The wetter the line got, the heavier it became and the harder it became to heave over.

But we didn't think of giving up. Not once. Every time we thought the same thing.

We'll go again. We'll go again.

As we regrouped and prepared to make another attempt, the interpreter once again explained the plan and what the skipper needed to do. But the message just didn't seem to be getting through. With every communication taking minutes rather than seconds, we were missing vital opportunities.

I waited for a third chance to line the boats up. When I spotted it, I radioed the coastguard to confirm my intention, then I moved alongside the yacht.

As the line was heaved across, I held my breath, willing the skipper to come out and grab it.

Once again, it simply flopped on deck.

Come on, I thought.

There was still time to grab it.

But nothing happened. The wind whipped the line off the deck and into the sea, and once more we were back to square one. As the lifeboat crew again swung into action, I shook my head. The delay in communication meant we were missing the window of a few seconds that we had to get the line over.

And we were running out of time.

Glancing nervously to the north, I could see we were moving closer and closer to the treacherous overfalls. Our Severn class lifeboat was now rolling dangerously in the waves as well.

We'd been trying to secure a tow for what seemed like hours and it just wasn't working. The yacht was drifting closer and closer to the shoal area of Outer Hurricane Rock. I had no choice but to start considering the worst-case scenario. If there was nothing we could do to stop the yacht heading out to the reef, we'd need to get the skipper off that yacht.

Did we get him to jump into the water? I thought.

One glance at the rising swell, and another at the frightened and exhausted sailor on the *Vestavind II*, told me that this wasn't an option. No. From where I was standing, there was only one way we'd be able to get the skipper.

We'd have to collide with the yacht and drag him off.

Bringing the boats into contact was risky and might compromise the lifeboat. There would be damage, for certain, and I had to think of the safety of my crew.

But it would save the skipper's life.

A knot formed in my stomach as I weighed up the options. I knew that the moment I needed to make a decision was looming. Colliding the boats was a last resort, but if I made that call the communication would have to be crystal clear.

Everyone would need to understand exactly what was going on.

Or we could end up with a man overboard.

And if the skipper went in, I didn't think we'd stand much chance of recovering him.

The thought played over and over in my mind as I came back around a fourth time. On deck, I could see one of the lifeboat crew gesticulating wildly at the skipper. Once again the tow was passed down the production line and just as I brought the lifeboat alongside the yacht, it was heaved over.

Catch the bloody rope!

Somehow, this time, the message got across.

I could have cheered as I saw the skipper edge out of the cockpit, grab the rope and quickly tie it to something on his stern – possibly a winch – before darting back to his cockpit.

Truth be told, it didn't look all that secure, but it was the best shot we had. I had to give it a try. Slowly, I began to tow the vessel away from the swell, stern first.

Please hold …, I thought.

Slowly, but surely, I felt the reassuring pull of the vessel as we moved away.

She's coming.

Gripping the helm, I continued moving forward, carefully and steadily. Every inch I moved was taking the yacht and our lifeboat away from the angry swell out in the shallows.

Away from that reef.

As we moved, my mind was already racing ahead. We had the boat on tow, but what next? Once we were clear of the reef we would need to transfer the tow to the bow. And after that ...?

Where on earth were we going to take him?

It was forty miles back to Islay. It had taken us more than two hours to get out here on our own. Towing a vessel, we'd have to go at a snail's pace, and in these conditions we'd never make it back to our home station without getting into more difficulties. Then I had a thought.

The Isle of Tiree.

Tiree was the most westerly island of the Inner Hebrides. It was relatively small – about twelve miles long by three miles wide – and very flat, with a famously mild climate.

It could provide some respite from these conditions.

It would mean going north, but if we went around the back of the island, where it was more sheltered, we could manoeuvre the lifeboat alongside the yacht, get the skipper off and abandon the yacht there, rather than trying to tow her all the way home.

After all, the yacht was insured.

Dealing with boats, we were often also dealing with people's livelihoods. People could be reluctant to abandon their vessels.

But a life was always more valuable than any boat ...

Suddenly, my thoughts were interrupted. I felt the weight go off the tow.

Oh no!

I didn't even need to look to know what had happened. The tow line had parted and it was now completely adrift from the yacht. We'd only been towing for five minutes.

I shan't repeat the words that rose up from crew on the life-boat deck. Let me tell you, the air was blue.

It felt like a complete disaster, but as I reassessed our position, I noticed what we'd done. We'd lost her again, but in the short distance we'd managed to tow her, we'd achieved something.

We'd pulled her far enough away from the overfalls to guarantee that she wouldn't get dragged onto the reef. She'd drift past and out into open water instead.

She was out of imminent danger.

In that moment I realised that we'd saved the skipper's life.

There'd be no need for any ramming or grabbing.

But there was no time to celebrate. The swell was still rising and there were hazards everywhere. The yacht and its skipper were safer, for sure. But they were still in danger. We had to try to secure the yacht again.

The crew began to regroup, a well-oiled machine by this point. Once the tow line was ready to go, I powered towards the yacht, aiming to get as close as possible so the crew could easily pass the line over.

But just as we drew alongside, a huge wave about fifteen metres high rose up above us. Almost as suddenly as it appeared, it crashed down on the yacht and the lifeboat. We felt the full force of the water collapsing on us.

'Woah,' I heard Duncan shout. He'd been standing in the doorway of the wheelhouse and I could tell he'd felt the impact too.

I clutched the wheel as we were tossed around violently. In the confusion, I saw the yacht bouncing towards us and gasped.

We were going to …
THUD!
Before I even had time to react, the stern of the lifeboat collided hard with the yacht's bow. Shockwaves ran through both boats. But miraculously, the collision presented an unexpected opportunity. As the two boats came into contact, David grasped what might have been our last chance and physically passed the tow line over to the skipper.

To my amazement, the skipper managed to grab it.
We were back in with a chance!
Without the looming worry of getting sucked towards the overfalls, the lifeboat crew were able to gesture and indicate to the skipper where the tow would be more secure. This time, he managed to attach the tow rope more securely to his vessel.

It was a glimmer of hope in a shout that had presented so many unexpected obstacles.

Losing the radar, the sickness, the language barrier, the shoal …
Finally, it felt like something was going our way. By now, it was half past six in the morning and we'd only been able to tow the yacht a few hundred metres. Granted, they were a life-saving few hundred metres, but there was still much more to be done.

I started to pull away again, but just as soon as I thought things were looking up, the relentless weather and gale-force winds snatched away our golden opportunity.

Moments after I started to move, the tow failed again.

This time, my heart truly sank.

We'd used all four of the heaving lines from the lifeboat. As I watched the yacht start to drift away again, with the skipper's face completely ashen, I knew we were out of options.

We needed help.

I radioed the coastguard and explained the situation.

'Belfast Coastguard, this is Islay Lifeboat,' I said. 'Assistance requested.'

'Assistance is on its way,' the coastguard confirmed.

Unknown to us, while we were battling to get the yacht under tow, a pipe-laying survey vessel called *Deep Energy* had heard our communications on the emergency frequency and they'd offered to assist.

'Stand by until *Deep Energy* arrives,' the coastguard instructed.

The vessel was still a few hours away, but with the yacht and its skipper safely away from the main swell, we knew that they wouldn't come to grief. All we had to do was wait and be on hand in case the situation shifted.

As we held our position, the coastguard informed us that RNLI Barra Lifeboat Station had also been requested to launch its all-weather lifeboat to come and relieve us.

'You've been out a long time,' the coastguard said. 'They can come and take over from you.'

It was music to my ears. Getting the yacht back to shore was going to be a long and challenging ordeal. My crew had done a tremendous job, but after battling with gale-force winds, sleet and rain for more than six hours, they were exhausted.

It would be far safer for Barra and *Deep Energy* to take over. However, we still couldn't sit back and relax. Holding position in seas as wild as these was no mean feat. Every moment, as we rolled in the swell, we had to watch where the waves were coming from and where they might take us, remaining vigilant for new dangers at all times.

At 11am, four hours after we'd called for back-up, I was finally able to heave a huge sigh of relief.

'Here she is,' I said, as a vessel came into view. It was *Deep Energy*, accompanied by *Rescue 100*, who had refuelled at its base in Prestwick and returned to assist. Barra lifeboat wasn't far behind, either, despite punching into the weather.

Our reinforcements had arrived.

The wind was still howling at gale force 8, and our lifeboat was being thrown around by the waves. Despite her size, even *Deep Energy* wasn't immune to the motion. It was quite a sight seeing her being tossed this way and that, but she was much more capable of sticking firm. As her captain skilfully manoeuvred the 195-metre vessel alongside the yacht and our lifeboat, the sea conditions transformed. Its huge bulk provided a lee for the strong winds.

A shelter blocking the gales.

It was like a brand new day. The waves dropped and our lifeboat steadied immediately. Suddenly the area was quiet and tranquil. We could have left immediately, but after almost twelve hours out at sea, we wanted to be ready to assist if the two boats needed us.

We wanted to see the job through to the end.

As the fresh crews swung into action, it emerged that one of the crew on *Deep Energy* was also a volunteer crew member at RNLI Buckie Lifeboat Station, on the Moray Firth on the east coast of Scotland. Using his RNLI training, he coordinated the transfer of the skipper over to *Deep Energy*. Safe in the lee of the huge ship, they were able to drop a ladder down the port side of *Deep Energy* and help the skipper aboard.

Everything happened in the nick of time. By the time the skipper was safely on board *Deep Energy*, about two minutes after back-up arrived, the yacht had already drifted out of the safety of the lee the ship had created. Back out in rough seas, it was thrashed about in the waves once again.

In relieving us, the Barra Lifeboat had been tasked to recover the vessel and tow it to safety, but after a few failed attempts conditions became too risky. Barra coxswain, Donald Macleod, made a decision.

'It's too dangerous to recover the yacht in these conditions,' he said. 'I don't want to put anyone in unnecessary danger.'

With the skipper now safe and well, and being winched into the coastguard helicopter from the deck of *Deep Energy*, I agreed wholeheartedly with the coxswain's call. The vessel could wait.

The shout might have been done and dusted, but our journey was far from over. Before we started back towards Islay, I spoke to the Barra boys over the radio.

'We're going to start heading home,' I said.

'Oh God,' said one of the Barra crew said. 'You're going to have one eye open on the journey home.'

'Tell me about it,' I said.

After being tossed and pushed every which way, we were now sixty miles from Islay Lifeboat Station. The minute we were out of *Deep Energy*'s lee, we were back into the weather, bouncing straight out of the water.

With strong winds and heavy seas continuing to batter us, I knew we couldn't just take the straight route home. We needed a course that would give us a little shelter and respite from being rattled around like coins in a can. I wasn't sure any of us had the energy for that.

'We'll get behind Tiree and shelter there,' I said to Thomas. 'Then we can nip straight across to the south of Mull, then right down behind Jura.'

'OK,' said Thomas.

It was the long way back, but I knew it would be quicker overall. Not to mention a heck of a lot more comfortable.

'Let's get home,' I said.

It was twenty past six in the evening when we were finally back on land at Islay – eighteen hours after we had launched. Throughout the whole job, the conditions had been so bad that we'd had to have our wits about us from start to finish. There had barely been a moment's rest.

We were physically and mentally exhausted.

Unsurprisingly, there wasn't any of the chat you'd usually have after a shout. We were all just absolutely knackered. And the sensation of walking on solid ground after so long out at sea?

It was quite the experience.

'This is weird,' said Duncan as we stepped onto the lifeboat station pier. 'I can't tell what's real.'

When we got into the station it was a hive of activity. The press had got wind of the drama and were after video footage that we'd captured from the camera on the boat.

I understood the interest, but I wasn't having any of it.

'I'm going to my bed,' I said.

When I returned to the station the next day, I learned that after a check-up the skipper had been given a clean bill of health. The *Vestavind II* was recovered that day by another fishing vessel, in calmer and safer conditions.

In the weeks after the shout, we followed all our usual processes, completing reports and accounts of the night. I even spoke to our regional inspector. I talked him through everything we did and even explained the other scenarios I'd considered.

Like colliding with the yacht and grabbing the skipper.

'Aye,' he agreed. 'We'd have accepted that as an option.'

It was good to know that my decision-making process had been sound. Before our meeting was wrapped up, the inspector turned to me.

'Just so you know, this rescue's going up to a panel,' he said. 'The one that decides on awards.'

'Oh right. OK,' I said.

To be honest, I was a bit taken aback. In thirty years of serving with the RNLI, I couldn't recall another service I'd been on being put forward for medal recognition. It was just never something I'd aimed for.

And when I found out I was going to be awarded the RNLI's Bronze Medal for Gallantry, I was stunned. My four crew members were also to be recognised with framed Letters of Thanks from the RNLI chairman. Rightly so – they'd all been marvellous.

Martin Porter, the captain of *Deep Energy*, his crew member and RNLI Buckie volunteer Gavin, and the pilot of the coastguard helicopter *Rescue 100* also received letters of thanks for their part in the rescue.

The presentation took place a little over a year after we'd gone out on the rescue. It was made in front of more than 120 people at Bowmore Village Hall in Islay – quite a gathering for an island with just over 3,000 inhabitants!

After receiving my medal, I said a few words. I was keen to express how the rescue had been an exceptional team effort, not just on the Islay lifeboat, but working with *Deep Energy* and RNLI volunteers from Barra and Buckie as well.

'I might have been the one making the decisions and helming the boat,' I said. 'But this was undoubtedly a fantastic team effort, with the crew on the deck doing the hard work.'

I also thanked all the shore and operations staff, and our fundraisers as well. You see, they always made everything the crew did possible, ensuring we were safe and supported, and that we had the best possible boats and equipment to serve our community.

Without any one of these elements, from the fundraisers who raised the money for our all-weather lifeboat and the shore crew that maintained her, to *Deep Energy* and the boys from Barra who wrapped up the whole ordeal, that rescue might not have happened. Up in the islands, we worked together and we looked after one another.

As for the teamwork displayed by RNLI Islay – well, it had been second to none. Just like it always had been and like it still is today. Everyone has their strengths and skills, everyone knows their role. They get on with it and do a bloody good job. No matter what you end up going out on, you're all in it together. You suffer the same conditions, you pull together and you do whatever needs to be done. I'm sure it's the same in RNLI stations across the country, but I'm particularly proud of our team here at Islay. They're an absolute credit to the service.

Over the course of thirty years with the RNLI, I've had a lot of memorable shouts – and this one is certainly up there. I know that a lot of the younger crew relish going out on rough nights like this. I was the same when I first joined the crew. But I turn fifty this year. My days of getting excited to be heading out in a rough night, they're gone now. Especially after going out for the *Vestavind II*. Nowadays, flat and calm does me just fine. I'm getting too old for bouncing about in boats!

3.

FURTHEST LIMITS

Mark Taylor-Gregg, Tynemouth 2015

It was a day like any other. Looking out of the window on the fifth floor of the lighthouse, the sea was calm. Gentle waves caused the boats in the quay to bob up and down against the backdrop of an intense blue sky, punctuated with wisps of white.

It was the perfect scene, tranquil but still filled with life. I positioned my camera carefully, then pressed the button.

I'll paint that, I thought at the click of the shutter.

As a seascape artist, the view from the High Lighthouse in Tynemouth was fertile ground for capturing moments in time just like this one, ready to immortalise them on canvas in oil or acrylic.

With the picture I'd just taken nearby, I picked up my brushes and started to paint. Absorbed in the moment, I slipped into my own world. Until suddenly, the peace was shattered by a familiar high-pitched, repetitive beep. It was coming from downstairs.

BEEP BEEP, BEEP BEEP.

Quick as flash, I ran down nine flights of stairs and through an open door.

'What's happened?' I said.

'A boat's stranded,' said Dallas. 'We're going to have to launch the lifeboat.'

Moments later, Margot appeared. Both of them were already in their RNLI crew uniform and clutching their helmets. The word 'Tynemouth' was emblazoned on the right-hand side of their shirts, just above the RNLI flag. Below it, the words 'crew' and '2B'.

Tynemouth RNLI crew to be.

You see, Dallas and Margot were my children, aged seven and six respectively, and they were playing in our living room, which was six floors directly below my studio.

I was an RNLI crew member and my kids had grown up seeing me go out on the lifeboats. They loved nothing more than to play make-believe that they were going out on a shout too.

And I loved getting involved …

My wife Pip and I had bought them all the pretend gear, right down to the RNLI wellies. Even the youngest, four-year-old Aurora, had her own kit, although she often played the part of the casualty, as she was doing now, standing on the other side of the room, pretending to bail water out of an imaginary boat.

'Help!' she shouted.

'You're going to need to tow her,' I said to her brother and sister.

'I'll get the rope,' said Margot, running off into another room.

'I'll prepare the lifeboat,' said Dallas.

They knew the drill. I couldn't help but laugh as I watched them pretend to tow her to safety.

Living right next to the mouth of the River Tyne, where it flowed out into the North Sea, boats and water were a big part of the fabric of our lives. I had a yacht, a motorboat and even a little dinghy with an outboard motor, in which I took the children out all the time, wearing their little lifejackets. I'd teach them how to drive it – always supervised of course. All three of them loved being on the water and they were forever asking me: *Daddy, when can we go on the lifeboats?*

They were just like I was at their age.

Growing up, my dad, Dallas Taylor, Mam June and my sister Isobel and I lived in Blyth, just up the coast from Tynemouth. My dad was a seascape artist, pilot-boat skipper and volunteer lifeboat crew at RNLI Blyth Lifeboat Station. It was my mam's doctor, Reg Carr, who got him involved. Mam was pregnant with my big sister Isobel and had gone in for a check-up. Reg knew of my dad from his work and saw his chance.

'Do you think Dallas might be interested in coming down the boat?' he'd asked.

'I'm sure he would be,' Mam replied. She didn't even need to ask. She knew what his answer would be.

And that was that.

Reg and my dad grew close. The bond you built up on the lifeboats was special. He ended up being my godfather, and he was a supporter of my dad's artwork too, even hanging a picture he painted in the waiting room of his surgery – the

Winston Churchill, a Watson class lifeboat that had been stationed at Blyth in the 1970s.

Dad had always been about the sea and the boats, even before he joined the crew at Blyth. I guess that's where I got it from. For as long as I can remember, I wanted to be just like my dad.

Even when he and my mam moved to Whitley Bay, he stayed crew on the lifeboats. He was over there all the time. He'd work carrying pilots to and from ships on his boat, which was berthed on one wall of the harbour. The slipway for the lifeboats was on the other. Between shifts, he'd sit in the watch house and paint local scenes – fishing boats and things like that. When I was there, he'd teach me how to paint in his style. We'd sit there for hours, just observing and painting together.

No matter what he was doing, he was always on call for the RNLI. It was a great thing to be around as a little kid. We would be in the car, driving around the town, when Dad's pager would go off. I'd be bursting with excitement as we drove to the station. Someone would call my mam to let her know where I was, but I wouldn't want to go home.

I wanted to be in the centre of it all.

I'd be in awe watching Dad getting his gear on and running towards the boat. Back then, the station had a Rother class lifeboat called *Shoreline* that needed to be launched down the slipway. My heart would be racing as the crew boarded the boat and the shore crew would knock the holding chain away.

The boat would roll down the slip and when it hit the water …

SPLASH!

VRROOOOMMM!

It would roar off to sea.

I loved that moment of impact. It gave me goose bumps every time. Whenever I saw it, all I could think was, *When I'm old enough, I'm going to do that. I'll be part of the crew.*

Over the years, Dad went out on some extreme rescues. He told me about some, but he was a humble man. More often than not it was other people telling me about the amazing things he'd done. Especially Mam. She was so proud of him.

She told me about one occasion when they'd been out on a shout in December 1982, towing a fishing vessel called *Castle Cove* to the Tyne, with three people on board. They reached the bar at the pier end but the conditions were awful, the confused sea tossing them about everywhere. The boat they were towing was suddenly flipped over, so the hull was upside down.

'It was your dad that cut that tow rope,' she said proudly. 'So they could go back and get them safely.'

They'd circled back and picked up the crew from the stricken vessel, who'd been hanging on to the upturned boat as it started to sink. The rescue even received recognition from the RNLI medals committee. The coxswain had been awarded a Bronze Medal and all the crew involved got a bronze certificate, including Dad.

'He's a real hero, your dad,' people would tell me. I agreed wholeheartedly. He was *my* hero, after all.

And my inspiration too.

He was on crew for twenty-six years, going down the mechanic route. After that, in 1996, he retired from boat crew and became the deputy launching authority for Blyth, on standby to make the decision if the coastguard requested that a lifeboat be launched. It was a huge responsibility, but there was no one as committed as my dad.

As I grew up, my career took me towards boats, but away from the sea. After I finished school, I ended up doing a degree in art and design at York St John University. My dad opened up a shop called The Studio in the Gateshead Metro Centre, where he could showcase and sell his artwork. He'd sit in the window of his unit and paint pictures from photographs that people sent him of their boats or of the beautiful coastline.

His customers loved his work because it was so intricate. His intimate knowledge of the sea and all that sailed upon it meant he brought flat snapshots to life, creating paintings that you felt you could walk into.

While I was at university, he let me paint alongside him in the shop. Most of his work was to order, and he always had a twelve-month waiting list, but I created pieces that people could buy there and then.

'Do you like that?' my dad would say, if he spotted someone looking at one of my paintings.

'It's lovely,' the customer would say.

'That's one of my son's,' he'd say, filling with pride. 'You can buy that now.'

And more often than not, they would. The extra money was handy and it helped me build up a network of people who liked my art. But most of all, I just loved spending time with Dad.

After university I got a job as a boat designer for a company called Sealine in Kidderminster. It was a dream job, building luxury motor yachts, but once again I was landlocked.

I stuck it out for a while, but slowly I moved back towards the north-east coast. I started as a lecturer in fine art and interior design at a local college and worked my way up into a management position. I moved to Cullercoats at first, near its inshore RNLI station. It was twenty minutes' drive from Blyth RNLI Lifeboat Station, but less than ten minutes from Tynemouth RNLI Lifeboat Station.

So close you could smell the salt from the sea.

Back in the day, Blyth had been an all-weather lifeboat station, but over time it became an inshore station, to best suit the needs of its local community. Tynemouth, on the other hand, had a new D class and the new Severn class, to replace the old Arun class. The Severn class could travel at twenty-five knots, meaning the station could cover a much larger patch than before.

At the time, the crew was full, but they were always training up new people, to meet demand and fill spaces as people retired and moved on. I relocated to Tynemouth Village to be closer to the station, and with more time on my hands, I became provisional lifeboat crew at Tynemouth in 2007, at the age of twenty-eight. It was later than I'd imagined, but I'd finally done it.

Michael Nugent, the station coxswain, and Kevin Mole, the mechanic at the time, welcomed me with open arms. They knew my dad, like everyone along that stretch of coast did. They often told me stories they'd heard about him, when I went along on exercises with them to learn about how they worked.

It always felt great to be Dallas K. Taylor's lad.

I did all my basic training, and practised and practised with them for six months. Then, one day, a space opened up on the crew.

'Are you up for joining us, Mark?' Michael asked.

'I most certainly am,' I replied, fighting to contain the exuberant excitement of the eight-year-old who had watched the lifeboats for years and imagined being an RNLI crew member.

It was all my childhood dreams come true. The day I had my letter through the post to say I'd passed my medical, I went straight to pick up my pager from Tynemouth RNLI Station. After that, I visited my parents' home in Whitley Bay.

'Mam, Dad, I passed my medical,' I said, as soon as I burst through the door.

'Well done, son,' Dad said. 'I'm not surprised, though.'

'He's been training you up to be on the crew since you were five years old,' Mam added with a smile.

It had been his plan all along.

'I had you berthing my boat in the harbour and doing those man-overboard exercises, so if I ever fell in, you or Isobel would be able to turn the boat around and rescue me,' he chuckled. 'I wanted you to be able to radio the coastguard for help from my fellow crew on the lifeboat.'

Now I was part of that crew, ready to help Dad or anyone else who might need assistance.

As the years passed, I progressed through the ranks. In 2010, two years after I got my pager, I was made helm. I'd taken a different path to my dad. I had my eye on the coxswain route rather than going for mechanic like he'd been, but he was pleased as punch with me.

I'd hear him sometimes, telling his friends about me.

'See there? That's my son,' he'd say. 'Following in his dad's footsteps on the lifeboats.'

I'd flush with pride every time.

They were big footsteps to follow. Dad finally retired from his deputy launching authority role on his seventieth birthday, after forty years' service. Not long after, at the Northern RNLI conference held at York Racecourse, he was presented with a special statuette to recognise his long service. It was the summer of 2010. Me, Mam and Isobel watched with tears in our eyes as he received the award, acknowledging his time on crew and support to the management of Blyth Station after his retirement from crew.

Despite the slightly later start to my lifeboat career, I felt like I was making up for lost time. Balancing work, my art and the lifeboats never felt like a chore. I was part of something special that Dad and I shared, and I was giving back to the community too. I'd never been happier.

Then a few months after the conference, we received some terrible news. Dad had been unwell for a little while, struggling to get around and losing weight, so he'd been to the doctor's for some tests. The diagnosis was unexpected and devastating.

He had motor neurone disease.

It took hold quickly. Watching such a physically and emotionally strong man, my rock and hero, wither away before our very eyes was heart-breaking. In fact, the last time he'd been able to walk unaided had been when he'd collected his long-service statuette award.

After all the years of love and support he'd given me, there was only one thing for it. I became his main carer. Mam was sixty-two herself, so she couldn't look after him alone. We knew that he didn't have long, and I wanted to do something to repay him for looking after me my whole life, to ensure he had his dignity right to the end. Moving around, swallowing and even breathing quickly became difficult for him. Poor Dad never did get to see much of his retirement. On 31 January 2011, six months after his diagnosis, he passed away.

The news spread quickly. We were overwhelmed by the outpouring of love for him. Even the local newspaper reported on his passing, asking me to share a few words about my dad. I had no idea where to start.

How could I put everything he'd given me into words?

'He was inspirational. He was a hero to everyone. He was a very generous and caring person,' I said. 'He was my best friend. He was my rock in terms of his advice and guidance, and I am incredibly proud to be his son.'

It was barely a snippet of everything I felt, but it did the job.

The next day, the story appeared in the paper. They'd used a fantastic photo of my dad, from his early days with the RNLI.

He was looking slightly off-camera and his lips were curled up into a slight smile. Hair and beard windswept, he was proudly wearing his RNLI lifejacket, with 'assistant mechanic' written over the left breast in permanent marker. He looked strong, happy and at ease.

Just how I wanted to remember him.

I choked up as I read the words that had been contributed by the RNLI. Andy Clift, our divisional inspector, paid tribute to Dad's work as a volunteer over the years: 'The RNLI couldn't exist without people like Dallas, who spent much of his life trying to help others,' he said. 'His enthusiasm for the lifeboat service has been passed on not just to his son Mark, but also to countless others whose lives he touched over the years.'

We laid him to rest on 8 February, the day that would have been his seventy-first birthday. His coffin was draped with the RNLI's flag, and a white seafaring cap was placed on top. It was a special service that honoured his longstanding commitment to saving lives at sea.

Over the years he'd rescued sixty-five people.

Sixty-five people who'd gone on to live full lives, have families and fulfil their dreams. All because of my dad.

As we gathered to celebrate his life at Blyth RNLI Lifeboat Station after the service, surrounded by hundreds of his friends, family and colleagues, I was heartbroken, but also filled with love and pride. I'd always wanted to emulate Dad. Now that drive was even stronger. I had his reputation to uphold and his legacy to continue.

It was a huge turning point in my life.

In the months that passed, I left college completely and committed myself to completing my dad's bulging order book. He'd trained me up in his style, so I knew I could fulfil his outstanding orders. I used all the skills he'd taught me, but I tried to see the pictures through his eyes as well.

Shortly after, I met the woman who would become my wife, a fellow artist called Philippa Gregg, or Pip for short. We had an instant connection and things moved fast. Four months into the relationship, I'd moved in with her and she was pregnant with our first child.

Pip lived in the High Lighthouse above North Shields Fish Quay. Designed for Trinity House and completed in 1808, it had been decommissioned as a working lighthouse in the 1990s, after which it was transformed into a private dwelling. The big white building was still used as a day navigation mark, however, because you could see it from twenty miles out. If you lined it up with the Low Lighthouse, lower down in the quay, you'd know you were right through the middle of the piers.

It was six minutes' walk from Tynemouth Lifeboat Station and gave me a great vantage point for my paintings, as well as for spotting potential trouble at sea. From the moment I moved there, I was forever at my windows, looking up and down the river, always anticipating something happening.

What's that in the water? A boat? A person?

I was just like Dad used to be when we'd sit painting together in the harbour.

Always on call.

Being so close, whenever there was a shout, I was one of the first down to the station. Even when our little boy arrived in 2012.

'Let's call him Dallas,' I said. 'After my dad.'

'It's perfect,' she said.

She'd never met Dad, but she knew all about him. I loved telling her the stories of all his rescues, and she loved hearing about them. What's more, she knew immediately how much the lifeboats meant to me. We could be out having a nice meal or be fast asleep in the middle of the night, but if the pager went off, she knew I'd be out the door and off to the station – and she supported me.

If I was rummaging around trying to find my socks or keys, she'd be there handing them to me, helping me to get on my way more quickly. Before I left, there was only one thing I had to do.

'I love you,' I'd say, planting a kiss on her lips.

'I love you too,' she'd reply.

I'd say the same to the kids and kiss them on their heads, then I'd be off. Our relationship was just like my mam and dad's. I felt lucky to have found someone so in tune with my life and loves.

When Dallas was four months old, Pip and I got married, and all the crew came up in an old Routemaster bus. She went from having nothing to do with the lifeboats to being part of the family.

It took a while, but I finally worked through Dad's order book. I'd always insisted that I wouldn't be a commercial artist, and that I'd just finish all Dad's orders and shut up shop. But doing this didn't feel commercial. It felt intimate and special.

I was continuing Dad's legacy.

I decided to carry it on. It made me feel close to Dad. I could work from home and be right next to the lifeboat station, on call all the time.

Just like Dad was.

Margot arrived not long after Pip and I married, and then in 2015 we found out that she was expecting again. Life certainly was busier with two young children and one on the way. Especially since I'd started my RNLI navigation training. Between us we managed, though. With the exception of a few days' training down at RNLI headquarters in Poole, I was usually at home, so we'd divide and conquer. In the morning, one of us would be on nappy duty, the other on breakfast.

That was exactly how it was on the morning of Wednesday, 24 June. I was knee-deep in nappies, and busy getting Dallas and Margot ready to go down for breakfast. Then at 9.30am, a familiar sound interrupted our morning routine.

Do do do do do do.

It was my RNLI pager.

I have to go.

The children were so used to the sound that they didn't even flinch, but Pip heard it from downstairs. Before I'd even turned to call her, she was there.

'I'll take over here,' she smiled.

'Thank you,' I said, leaning over to kiss Dallas and Margot.

'See you later,' I said to them both. As I brushed past Pip, I patted her bump and kissed her.

'Love you,' I said.

'Love you too,' she replied.

I bolted down the stairs, grabbed my jacket and keys from their place by the door, and ran out to the car. Within minutes I was at the station and through the doors, looking down at my pager to see what kit I needed.

Launch ALB.

We were going out in the all-weather lifeboat, so I'd need

my all-weather gear on. Jacket, boots, helmet – the lot. As we got ready, details about the shout circulated. Apparently, at 6am the Humber coastguard had received a call from the lone skipper of a fishing boat called the *Louise Thomsen*, which was taking on water.

The coastguard's local rescue helicopter had been scrambled and its winchman had lowered a salvage pump down, so the skipper could stem the flow of water. The risk of sinking and the boat's heading, speed and current position had been taken. Once the skipper confirmed the situation was under control, the helicopter had returned to base to refuel and the coastguard had requested that our all-weather lifeboat be launched to go bring the vessel in.

A tow job, I thought. *Simple enough.*

Michael, the station coxswain, got the crew's attention.

'Right, this is going to be a big shout,' he said. 'If you have to work or need to be back, stand aside. This is going to be a long one.'

When we usually had a long shout, it would be thirty miles or so offshore. Four or five hours there and back, tops.

But it turned out that the *Louise Thomsen* was over a hundred miles off the coast. That would mean a good four or five hours just to get to her.

Never mind getting her back in.

People stood down one by one, until just a handful of us remained.

'You sure you're OK for this?' Michael asked each of us.

'I'll be fine,' I said, when my turn came. 'My wife's got the kids.'

I was self-employed, working as an artist from home. I could pick up the palette knife or the brush when I got back. My paintings weren't going anywhere. What's more, I wanted to try out my new training. I'd done a few exercises in the short time since I'd come back from Poole, but this would be the first real shout I'd be the navigator on.

'It'll be a challenge for me,' I said. 'A good way to test my navigator skills.'

Fresh back from training, it had been a given that I would take the navigator seat on the next shout.

Satisfied that everyone understood the scale of the job, we boarded the lifeboat and took our positions. There were six seats in the wheelhouse of the Severn class boat. As coxswain, Michael took the one in the middle. To his left was the wheel. George Jasper, the helm and deputy coxswain, took up his place there, and I sat to his right, at the navigation table. I flicked on the navigation system and it whirred to life. Up popped the message that always appeared.

This is an aid to navigation. This is not a primary source.

It wasn't like following the satnav in your car. To navigate at sea, you needed to be able to do it manually as well, using charts and coordinates of latitude and longitude.

Brian McDonald, the mechanic, slipped into his seat behind me.

Where Dad would have sat, in his role.

Brian had all the dials and gauges for the engine, temperatures and fuel in front of him. Above him were the radios: a VHF or very high frequency radio, which we used to communicate with the coastguard and the station, a medium-wave and a long-wave radio. As I got myself settled, the radio crackled into life.

It was the coastguard confirming the details of the shout: 'We've had a report to say fishing boat the *Louise Thomsen* is taking on water. She's a decommissioned Danish trawler. These are the coordinates of her last known position.'

I scribbled down the numbers on the notepad on my desk, then put the coordinates into the boat's navigation system, along with direction and speed. As the computer did its thing, I did mine.

Taking heed of the system's warning and remembering my training, I began plotting the route manually using the chart.

She's going from there. Heading in that direction. So if she's along that line, it should take us about …

After a few calculations, I had it.

'Our ETA is four and a half hours,' I said.

'ETA to the *Louise Thomsen* four and a half hours,' Brian said into the radio.

By working out all of the factors that would have impacted the boat since the coastguard helicopter left her, I'd worked out her EP, or estimated position. Once I had that, I could calculate how long it would take us to get there. The navigation system had estimated the same too.

They were more than reliable, but we all knew that even the best technology could fail. That's why everything that went into the system went down on the chart and the notepad too. If anything failed, we'd still know exactly where we were, and where we were going.

Course plotted, we started our journey. According to the coordinates given to us by the coastguard, the small fishing boat was actually 110 nautical miles off the coast in an area called the Dogger Bank in the middle of the North Sea.

Like searching for a needle in a haystack.

We were on our way. But we couldn't just kick back and relax until we got there. I had to pay attention to detail the whole way. I was repeating the same processes every fifteen minutes, checking our location and plotting it on the chart as we went along, recalculating our ETA with every shift and change, as well as constantly scanning for dangers on the radar.

The words of Pete Gale, my trainer at RNLI HQ, rang in my ears.

Plot your course.

Check the radar.

Scan for the casualty [jargon for a stricken vessel].

Look out the window.

Have a sip of coffee.

Then do it all again.

'We're not able to achieve twenty-five knots in these waves,' Michael said.

'OK,' I said, going back to my charts and recalculating the journey.

Changes could shave minutes off a journey or add time on. Sometimes a little, sometimes a lot. It all got logged.

Made contact with Humber coastguard.

Plotted course to EP.

Confirmed ETA to Humber coastguard.

Reduced speed to twenty-two knots.

It was a complete timeline of our journey, recording what happened – an analogue version of a plane's black box, if you like.

'Let's check what we're doing here,' Michael said, looking over my shoulder at the chart. As coxswain, it was his job to oversee what I was up to. I held my breath momentarily. I was confident, but it was my first time out as navigator. I could practically see the cogs turning in his head as his eyes darted from chart to navigation system to notepad.

'Yeah, that's fine,' he said, after what felt like an eternity.

'Great,' I said, heaving a sigh of relief.

An hour passed, then two. By now we were already far from the familiar scenery of the coast, away from the small fishing boats and way past the mouth of the River Tyne.

We were even out of range for the VHF radio, and had to switch to the medium- and long-wave radio, connecting us to the offshore shipping channels used by huge ships and tankers in the middle of the ocean.

And we weren't even halfway there.

Between plotting and checking, then plotting and checking again, there was enough space in the routine for a brew every now and again. We took turns to do rounds.

'Cuppa anyone?' I said, when it was my turn.

Five affirmative responses came back.

'Two sugars in mine,' said crew member Daniel Howe.

'Me too,' said Jonathan Jordan, another volunteer.

Goodness knows, we were going to need the energy.

After four or so hours, we neared *Louise Thomsen*'s estimated position. We were right on track and we knew that she could come into view at any moment.

Our eyes were trained on the miles and miles of sea in front of us, each scanning our particular vantage point for any sign of the trawler.

'I'll switch on the D/F,' George said, reaching up and clicking a button.

The D/F was the directional finder, a piece of kit that would give a vessel's bearing from us when they communicated with the lifeboat over the radio.

'*Louise Thomsen*, this is Tynemouth Lifeboat. Do you read me?' he said. We all paused and waited.

Silence.

'We're still not quite at the EP yet,' I said, patiently.

Michael nodded. 'We'll try again in a minute,' he said.

I continued at my desk. Poring over the charts and papers, I went over everything I'd noted down. Our route had been calibrated, checked and rechecked every fifteen minutes. It had been correct at the start and it was correct now. Half an hour later, we were exactly at the point where I'd expected her to be.

But there was nothing to be seen for miles.

George prompted us to give it another go with the directional finder.

'*Louise Thomsen*, this is Tynemouth Lifeboat. Do you read me? Over,' he said. Again, we all paused. Our patient silence extended into a heavy one.

'She should be here,' I said eventually, a knot forming in my stomach. When we'd set out, I'd hoped we would reach this point, send out the signal and get something back. Then all we had to do was get the skipper of the fishing boat to count down ten to one, so we could home in on the bearing and pinpoint exactly where she was.

Then we could get on with the job of bringing her home.

But after one long hour and several attempts with the directional finder, we were still met by silence.

The longer it went on, the heavier the atmosphere in the wheelhouse became, as the potential implications of the silence sunk in.

Had the boat got into further difficulties? Been washed off its course? Had it sunk?

We could even be looking for a person in the water, rather than a boat. My heart sank. The last thing any of us wanted this to turn into was a search-and-rescue mission. I took a deep breath as I started to choke up at the thought.

No, I thought, firmly. *We're not done yet.*

'Let's start the search plan,' I said, setting out our coordinates, just as I'd learned on my course. Using the technique I'd been taught, I plotted a box that showed where the fishing boat might be, based on everything from tidal changes to the effect of the wind. Once we had that, we had to search every inch of it.

We'd go along a leg to the end of the 'box', turn ninety degrees, travel the calculated track spacing, turn ninety degrees again, go back along a leg in the other direction …

Almost like mowing stripes up and down a lawn.

You did it over and over again, until you'd covered the lot. It was painstaking, but it did the trick. Usually our 'box' was reasonably small. But not today. Based on the boat's last known coordinates, she could be anywhere.

Like looking for a needle in a haystack, I thought again.

What's more, we had fuel to worry about as well. Search patterns consumed fuel. Being so far out, we had to make sure that we had enough to get us home – or we'd end up a casualty too.

In the RNLI, crew safety was paramount, and we always had to ensure ten per cent reserves were in our tank.

Brian checked the fuel gauges and did some calculations of his own.

'We have enough fuel for one search,' he said, finally.

The knot in my stomach pulled tighter. That meant there was no getting to the end and trying again. We were working at the limits of our search capacity.

This was our one chance.

We all focused. Each crew member was doing his job to the highest standard, with the sole aim of finding that boat and its skipper safe and well.

Trouble was, even as we followed the search pattern, we didn't know what we were looking for anymore. It was always going to be tough to spot her, a fishing boat bobbing around in the open sea.

But if she'd started to sink?

We could be looking for nothing bigger than a bow peeking above the waves.

Even bits of debris or a person in the water.

I shuddered at the thought.

Each leg of the search pattern took twenty minutes. As we powered up and down, we heard from the coastguard helicopter. It had refuelled and was heading back out to assist us. Using its elevated position, it threw its signal out far wider than we could. When we started the penultimate leg of the search pattern, my stomach started to churn. The wheelhouse was silent, no one wanting to say the words we were all thinking.

We aren't going to find her.

None of us took our eyes off the sea. But our hope was fading fast. Until suddenly, the radio crackled to life. We all listened, still watching the sea in front of us, searching for any sign that a boat had been there.

It was the helicopter pilot.

'Tynemouth Lifeboat, we've had a communication back from the vessel. Over,' he said.

'Yes,' I said, punching the air. Brian grinned at us as he took down all the details. When the communication was over, he relayed the news to us.

'They said the signal is very weak, but it's there,' he told us.

'What's her new estimated position?' I asked, scribbling down the numbers as he replied. After five hours of near silence, it was a joy to hear communications suddenly start to ping back and forth.

'*Louise Thomsen*, are you safe and well? Any injuries?' the helicopter asked.

'All well here. No injuries,' the skipper replied.

'Is the boat close to sinking?' came the next question.

'Still taking on water, but steady at the moment,' he said. He didn't sound too panicked.

'Can you give us your position?' the helicopter asked.

Pen poised, I took the coordinates down again, then plotted them on the chart.

He was thirteen miles further south than we'd expected him to be.

'What on earth happened there?' I said aloud.

Not that it mattered. I could have cried at the news. In fact, I don't think a single one of us didn't have a lump in our throats. We were right on the limit of our boat's capability, about to be forced to return to the station.

Then there it was. A ray of hope.

The boat wasn't lost.

And we weren't done yet.

After that boost, our training kicked in again. We went back to the process.

'OK,' I said, 'let's plot that position in.'

We'd gone from a huge search area to a position. A position that was accurate to a very short time before – not to eight hours earlier, like the first one we received.

'We're about an hour away,' I said.

'I've got that too,' Michael said.

'New course one-eight-zero,' I said to Michael, telling him the direction we needed to be travelling in.

'Steer one-eight-zero,' he relayed to the helm. As soon as we were on course, Michael turned to me again.

'Steering one-eight-zero,' he said.

Down it went on my timeline. Always checking, always logging. Always full of detail. Maybe my profession had something to do with why I enjoyed navigation. There was routine and ritual involved, and an almost obsessive attention to detail.

As we drew closer and closer to the new position, we observed the D/F closely. This time we got something back. Not radio contact, but a return signal that allowed us to tweak and hone our course towards her.

Soon we were in her vicinity.

The sea was rough and huge waves were rising up, tossing us around and dipping us into troughs, over and over.

Not ideal conditions for a boat that was taking on water.

'OK, let's keep our eyes open,' Michael said. 'Let's spot this vessel as soon as possible.'

Flanked by the helicopter above, we started our search again. We knew that if we didn't find her soon, she could be flipped over – or even go down.

Our brows furrowed, we scanned the water ahead of us, back and forth, back and forth, as we had been doing for hours.

Left, right. Left, right.

Our eyes scanned ahead and to the side. The motion of the waves was almost hypnotic, but I forced myself to focus. Then suddenly I sucked a deep breath in.

What was that?

It was a brief flash, but it was something – just to the right of the bow. Still holding my breath in, I waited to come over the next wave. As we did my heart almost leapt clean out of my chest.

'There she is! Off the starboard bow. One o'clock,' I shouted.

'Got her,' said Michael, as he caught sight of her as well.

But just as quickly as she appeared, she vanished again.

The sea didn't make things easy for us. We had to keep close tabs on the boat as we approached, keeping her in our eyeline and tracking slowly forward until, finally, we reached her.

Now we needed to get her home.

Before we could even think about moving her, we had to help slow the *Louise Thomsen*'s intake of water. With the helicopter still circling above us, George – the helm and deputy coxswain

– went up onto the deck with our salvage pump. It was too rough to transfer a member of crew over, vessel to vessel, but we could get the kit he needed over to him.

The boat could still move under her own power, so we could have escorted her, but we decided that towing her in would be the quickest and safest way to get her back to Tynemouth.

'We're going to pass a line over,' Dan informed the skipper.

'I'm coming out,' he replied.

He emerged onto the deck and waited, while George readied the line and tossed it over to him. He secured it to his bow and then returned down below to finish setting up the salvage pump.

We began to tow the vessel very slowly. Too much speed in this sea could capsize her. Then after a few minutes, the skipper's voice crackled through the radio.

'I can't get the pump working,' he said. 'I'm still taking on water.'

We all looked at one another. This wasn't good. We were attached, and if she went down …

She could take us with her.

'We're going to have to go on board,' Michael said.

'We won't get close enough for vessel to vessel,' George said.

'We'll use the Y-boat then,' Michael decided.

The Y-boat was a bit like the RNLI's D class lifeboat, but smaller – a bright orange, rigid inflatable boat that sat on top of the Severn class. It was there to be used for rescues close to rocks and other vessels, in places where the Severn class couldn't reach, or to be used in a worst-case scenario.

To rescue our crew if we put ourselves on the rocks.

George and Johnny Jordan swung into action, launching the Y-boat and motoring across the four-metre gap between our two vessels. George dropped Johnny off and returned in the Y-boat.

With Johnny on the *Louise Thomsen*, carrying his VHF radio, we suddenly had a better picture of the situation on board, not to mention how the skipper had come to be thirteen miles from his estimated position.

It turned out he'd discovered he'd take on less water if he changed course, so he decided to go further south. But his long-wave radio wasn't working properly, so he couldn't inform anyone. He just had to go for it.

Instead of hitting land at Sunderland, he would eventually have bumped up on shore in Norfolk.

Even with Johnny on the boat, our problems weren't over. The salvage pump wasn't working. The skipper had already been pumping out since 6am, when he'd raised the alarm with the coastguard. It was now around 3pm, almost nine hours later.

He was exhausted.

'We're going to have to revert to pumping out manually,' Johnny said over the radio. That meant getting to the lever for the vessel's bilge pump – a pipe running down to the bottom of the boat – and physically pumping the water out of the boat. Johnny and the skipper planned to alternate.

Twenty minutes on, twenty minutes off.

I began plotting our course back to the station. With a boat in tow in this sea, we could only travel at a fraction of the speed we'd come out at. We'd been doing twenty-two knots but now we had to drop it to six knots maximum.

After already being out for six hours – two hours longer than a normal 'long' shout – it was going to take us another twelve hours to get home.

And they were going to have to pump out the whole way.

I didn't envy them one bit.

Things were still intense over in our wheelhouse too. Towing a vehicle presented all kinds of risks. You had to battle with rope length, the pull and snatch.

You wanted your boat and the stricken vessel on top of the wave at the same time and coming down at the same time. If you went too fast, the vessel in tow could capsize or the tow could easily part and they could drift away from you. Keeping everything running smoothly required constant communication.

We checked in with Johnny every fifteen or twenty minutes.

'How's this speed, Johnny? Is it appropriate?' Michael asked.

'Tow all good. Speed is fine,' he replied.

Sometimes he'd ask us to slow down, sometimes to pick it up. It was all about tweaking and balance. Reacting to the waves and the weather.

It was hard work, but the mood on the lifeboat was much lighter. We still had a serious job to do, but we now knew that the skipper was safe and well, so we could heave a collective sigh of relief.

And have another cuppa.

'Who's for a brew?' I asked.

'Oh, yes please,' said George.

I cracked the biscuits out this time too. We deserved them. For the first time in hours we were able to relax, just a little.

Maybe it was because we were on our way back, but we started to chit-chat about what we should have been doing back home.

'Well, I've got out of doing the gardening,' Brian said.

We all laughed.

'The kids will have Pip up the wall,' I said. Although, really, I knew she'd have everything under control. That's why she and I worked so well. We were a team.

Over the next ten hours we maintained a steady routine. Although the pressure was off to a certain extent, we had to remain sharp and focused. Especially me, as a new navigator. I didn't want to make any mistakes.

Plot your time, plot your position.

Done.

Plot it on the paper chart. Put it in the computer.

Done.

Have a sip of coffee.

Done.

We had to keep our energy levels up too. If anything happened, a fatigued crew would be no use at all, and biscuits and chocolate bars alone wouldn't sustain us. Every few hours we'd tuck into a hot can – a kind of posh pot noodle, like astronauts have.

All the while we were aware that the situation on the *Louise Thomsen* could change at any minute. We're there to save lives at sea, not save boats at sea. If she started to capsize we'd have to cut the tow and get Johnny and the skipper off that boat, sharpish.

We also had the fuel situation to stay on top of. I couldn't remember a shout this far out, and fuel was bound to be running low. Realistically, we could never do anything that would end up with us running out of fuel, especially with us this isolated and far from rescue. So Brian checked his fuel gauges as anxiously as I checked my charts. We needed to get back with that ten-per-cent reserve.

'How are we looking for fuel?' I asked, as I saw him at his instruments, scratching his head.

'It's going to be tight, but we're doing OK,' he said.

The hours passed. When the north-east coastline came into view, ever so faintly in the distance, I was filled with a new burst of energy. Moving inshore, we switched from long-wave to medium-wave radio. Eventually, we switched back to VHF radio.

We were almost home.

Working on channel zero, the emergency frequency channel, we kept the communications formal.

'Tynemouth Lifeboat to Humber Coastguard, position is ETA 4.30am,' said Brian.

'Roger, Tynemouth Lifeboat,' came the reply from the coastguard.

We knew that our fellow crew members would be in the station, listening in. They'd be happy to hear we were on our way back in.

Just as I'd plotted every movement on our way out, I plotted all the way back in. By the time we got to Sunderland with the *Louise Thomsen* and released our lines, once she was tied up in the South Quay, I was counting every minute down to when we'd be home. After more than eighteen hours at sea, we were all mentally and physically exhausted.

It took us twenty minutes to get back into the Tyne. When

we arrived at the fuel berth, we were just shy of ten-per-cent fuel reserves.

Not bad, considering …

The job might have been over, but we still had to make the Severn class ready for service again. A new shout could come in five minutes after we returned. We refuelled her, washed her down to get any salt off the deck and restocked the boat's supplies.

The coffee jar and biscuit tin were looking considerably depleted.

With both fuel tanks almost empty, it took almost an hour to fill her up. Ordinarily there'd be some chat as we turned the boat around, but today was different. No one had any energy. After launching at 9.30am on Wednesday, 24 June, we had the boat back and ready for service at 5.30am on Thursday, 25 June.

'Great work today,' I said, as I pulled on my coat and grabbed my car keys from my locker. 'I'm off to bed.'

'Night, Mark,' came several tired responses.

I barely remember getting home and slipping into bed next to Pip. I think I must have been asleep as soon as my head hit the pillow.

Maybe even before.

The next thing I remember was hearing the kids stirring and Pip getting up to start our daily routine. I rubbed my eyes and looked at the clock. It was 7am.

'Morning,' said Pip with a smile. 'Coffee?'

It was music to my ears.

'Yes, please,' I said.

'Long job yesterday, wasn't it?' she said. All I could do was nod. I'd fill her in on all the details later, but right now we had other jobs to do.

Twenty-four hours after my pager had gone off, I was back to doing the nappies, and getting the kids dressed and ready for the day ahead. The lads that had employers would have headed out to work as normal. Michael, a fisherman, would have gone to check his pots, since he'd not been to them the previous day. We all just slipped back into normal life.

It was only later in the day that I realised just how significant the job had been. While we'd been offshore, the local paper had got wind of the shout and a story had even been published while we were still out at sea. There was a picture of our Severn class roaring out of the harbour, under the headline, *Tynemouth lifeboat crew spends over eleven hours at sea helping stricken vessel.*

We were barely past halfway by that point!

Suddenly it began to dawn on me that I'd been part of something quite epic. It was certainly the longest shout I'd ever been on. Asking the rest of the crew, none of them could remember a longer one in the station's history. We heard that – at a distance of 110 nautical miles – it was believed to be the furthest English shout on record for the RNLI. The previous record had been ninety-eight nautical miles, set by a crew at RNLI Valentia Lifeboat Station back in 1985. We were all astonished.

I couldn't help but think just how proud Dad would have been, me being a part of something like that. I could almost hear him.

'See that? That's my boy. Following in my footsteps.'

I still see my work with the RNLI as me continuing my dad's legacy. I want to serve our community as well as he did, and I want to give my kids someone to look up to and be proud of, like Dad did for me. Nothing would make me happier than if my mini crew in training chose to follow in mine and their grandad's footsteps too.

Five years on from the *Louise Thomsen* rescue, I've still never had a shout quite like that. It was a mental and physical challenge like no other. I've no idea if there has been an RNLI shout as far as ours, or the RNLI Valentia one in fact, but seeing it all as the navigator was a real eye-opener. It gave me great experience for the jobs that came after it.

I'm training up to coxswain now, a whole new role and perspective. I think my dad would be bursting with pride to think that I was going to be in command of the Severn class leaving Tynemouth Lifeboat Station.

I only have a few more assessments left to do now. Funnily enough, one of them is search and rescue. I'm sure I'll be drawing on the experience I gained on the *Louise Thomsen* rescue when that comes around!

4.

POINT OF NO RETURN

Darren Harcus, Lerwick 2017

The pager on my bedside table sprang to life, its high-pitched, repetitive beep echoing round the room and snapping me out of a deep sleep.

I was only a couple of days back on land after a two-week shift as crew on the fishing boat I worked on and I'd been sleeping like a log.

BEEP BEEP, BEEP BEEP.

I sat up, rubbed my eyes and looked at the clock. It was six-thirty in the morning. Grabbing the pager, I read the message on the screen.

Launch ALB.

The Severn class lifeboat at RNLI Lerwick Lifeboat Station was being sent out, and I needed to get down there quickly. As I climbed out of bed and started to rummage around for my clothes, the pager continued to sound.

BEEP BEEP, BEEP BEEP.

'Turn that thing off, will you?' my fiancée Gemma mumbled from beneath the duvet.

'Sorry,' I whispered, as I silenced it.

She was used to the pager going off at all hours. I'd been volunteer crew almost as long as she'd known me. She supported my involvement with the RNLI, but if I was awake and on my way, she was of the opinion that she didn't need to be listening to the beep.

Couldn't blame her at this time in the morning, I thought.

I bolted out of the house, jumped into the car and drove the mile down the road to the lifeboat station. Despite being there in minutes, I was the last one in.

We all moved fast when a shout came in.

As I burst through the doors and ran towards the changing area to get kitted up, I heard someone call my name.

'Darren,' said Iain Derbyshire, another member of volunteer crew.

'Yeah?' I replied, still running.

'It's your boat,' he said.

The words made me pull my kit on even faster than usual.

Then Alan Tarby, the coxswain, appeared. When he caught sight of me, he looked relieved.

'I'm glad to see you,' he said. 'I thought you might still be on there.'

On where …?

Then it hit me like a bag of cement.

On the *Ocean Way*.

The boat that we were going out to assist was the boat I'd been working on a couple of days earlier.

The one I'd worked on for the past five years of my life.

My stomach lurched. Ten of us worked on board, in rotating shifts. We were all great friends, so I knew exactly who would be on board.

I was always concerned for the crew of any stricken vessel we went out to. But this was different.

These were my friends and colleagues.

'What happened?' I asked, as we boarded our lifeboat, the *Michael and Jane Vernon*.

'We'll fill you in on the way out,' said Alan.

I'd been fishing professionally for almost twenty years. Growing up on Westray in Orkney, an archipelago in the Northern Isles of Scotland, it was natural to fall into coastal and sea-faring jobs.

As well as fishing, I'd volunteered for the Westray Auxiliary Coastguard before moving to Shetland in 2013. I'd started a job as crew on the *Ocean Way* in 2011, after one of my best friends asked if I'd be interested. She was an eighty-five-foot twin-rig fishing vessel that trawled for monkfish, or 'monks' as we called them.

The family that owned the boat had been in the business for several generations, but they'd launched the *Ocean Way* sometime in 2009 or 2010. It was a good job and the crew were very experienced. When I'd last been on board, at least three of us had been at sea since leaving school, boasting about sixty years' experience between us.

What's more, the money was great, and it was probably the easiest fishing job I'd ever had – at least, as easy as fishing could be!

Long hours exposed to the elements, physical exertion, and stretches of time away from family and friends could be tough, but most of the time I loved it.

We had two crews of five people rotating in shifts. We worked two weeks on, two weeks off. When you were on the boat it was hard graft, working for hours on end before heading down below to watch some TV.

Football was a favourite to watch during down time. Most of us were Aberdeen FC fans, but there were some rivalries. When it came to English football I supported Manchester United, while my friend Shaun Michie was an Arsenal fan, which often led to a friendly bet or two. If there was nothing good on the telly, we'd sit down and eat together or just grab a few hours' sleep. Anything just to unwind.

Although we'd try to land fish every three to four days, to make sure they were as fresh as possible, *we* wouldn't alight on land. Once we'd unloaded the catch, we'd be straight back out to sea.

Working out on the boats around the Shetland Islands, you became part of a small and close-knit community. Other trawlers and fishing boats, ferries and cargo ships – we'd all help one another out. Understanding the sea as we did, we knew how easy it could be to find yourself in difficulty. We all had each other's backs.

After all, you never knew when you might need the help returned.

Lending a hand made you feel like you were doing your part. But sometimes, no matter how much help came, we'd all be left helpless.

Every once in a while there would be an incident that would shake the whole community.

On Friday, 23 August 2013, I was working out at sea. It was a perfectly normal day, until news began to spread of an accident two miles west of Sumburgh Airport. First it came over the radio, then it was on our TV.

A helicopter carrying eighteen people back from one of the oil rigs had suddenly ditched in the sea. As always, our community swung into action. The local lifeboat crews launched, and helicopters from the coastguard and RAF Lossiemouth, along with two Bond rescue helicopters, were scrambled to search for survivors. Boats in the area that were not connected to the rescue services, including a ferry and a cargo ship, joined the search as well.

Fourteen people were rescued that night.

But four were lost.

Too far away to assist, we watched the TV helplessly as the incident played out on the news, with aerial footage of the wreckage and reports of survivors being rescued. Then the news of those lost and the recovery mission to find their bodies.

It was gut-wrenching.

The next day the story was all over the local and national news.

Shetland helicopter crash: four people confirmed dead by police.

It turned out that the helicopter experienced a catastrophic loss of power, dropping into the sea so suddenly that it didn't have a chance to make a controlled landing.

It had been down to the RNLI and other emergency services to recover the bodies and the clear the wreckage. RNLI Lerwick's crew brought two of the bodies back to Sumburgh. The charity's statement to the media echoed what we were all thinking.

'Obviously this is the news that everyone, including our lifeboat volunteers, dreaded,' the spokesperson said. 'Our thoughts and prayers are with the families and loved ones of those concerned.'

The feeling of helplessness stuck with me. If anything like that happened again, I wanted to know that I could be of use. That I might be able to make a difference.

I decided to join the RNLI, but it wasn't quite as simple as just turning up and filling in a form. I had to find someone who was already involved, or who had been in the past, to express my interest. I made some enquiries via my cousin, Robbie Stout, who pointed me in the right direction. His father-in-law, Bruce Leask, was the coxswain at Lerwick at the time.

'Go along and have a chat with him and the mechanic,' Robbie advised. After he mentioned my interest, I dropped in to see them and explain why I wanted to join. John Best was the then full-time mechanic.

After hearing me out, they agreed to take me on a few exercises. They wanted to see if I got on with the rest of the crew and if I could do the work. For about a year, I acted as provisional crew.

Then, finally, I got my pager.

I didn't have any aspirations to progress through the ranks at the time, I just wanted to be able to use my skills to make a difference. Plus, with my job on the *Ocean Way*, being volunteer crew suited me perfectly. I loved being out at sea, so what better way to spend my time off than being on call for the RNLI?

When I joined the RNLI, I never in a million years imagined that I'd be going out on a shout to rescue the vessel that I worked on.

Nor had I ever wanted to …

That said, since it *was* happening, I was glad that I was one of the people going out to help. I knew the crew and had detailed knowledge of the inner workings of the boat.

Another reason Alan was glad to see me, I thought.

Whatever was happening out there, I knew I had valuable intelligence that could help us out.

At quarter past seven we threw off the ropes and launched the lifeboat. There was a breeze running and a bit of a swell, but it was a clear morning and we were still making around twenty-five knots towards *Ocean Way*'s location, twenty-three miles away.

Despite making good progress, it was still going to take us forty-five minutes to get there, so Alan brought me up to speed on what they already knew. It turned out that the boat was about ten miles east of Out Skerries, a small cluster of islands that we often passed through.

'She's taking on water,' Alan explained.

'How's that happened?' I asked.

'Punctured the hull, apparently.'

'Is anyone standing by?' I asked, wondering if any local boats were helping them until we got there.

'There's a Norwegian fish carrier lending a hand. They've transferred a salvage pump over.'

Despite the damage, they were still making their way back towards Lerwick, which was a good sign. To someone with no knowledge of seafaring, the idea of a boat with a hole in it was worrying – and rightly so. But it did happen.

A few years earlier we'd had a bit of wear underneath the hull at the stern. We'd developed a small leak and had to manage it until we could berth and repair the damage. I imagined that this was a similar situation.

They'll be fine, I thought.

Just to be sure, though, I decided to phone *Ocean Way*'s skipper, Steven Hughson. Speaking to him directly, I'd get a better picture of how things were going. I'd be able to sense any real concern in his voice. I took my mobile out and dialled his number. After a couple of rings he answered.

'I'm on my way out on the lifeboat,' I said. 'How are you getting on?'

'It's all under control,' he replied. 'We're keeping up with the flow.'

'That's great,' I said. 'Let me know if anything changes.'

As I hung up, I looked at Alan and gave a nod.

'He seems OK,' I said.

'Great,' said Alan.

Like I mentioned, the crew were experienced and I knew they worked well together. Truth be told, it was a luxury going out on a shout and having that confidence.

They'll be fine, I thought again.

As we neared the vessel's location, the coxswain shared his plan. Helping the crew stem the flow of water into the boat was going to be a priority. We always had our salvage pump ready to go, in case a situation like this arose.

'Darren, when we arrive we'll get you onto the boat with John Best,' Alan said.

'OK,' I said.

'No problem,' John said.

It was a given that I'd be going over. Not just because of my relationship with the crew, but because he knew I'd manage whatever we were faced with calmly. I was good at staying steady in most situations. John, who'd been one of my ways onto crew and had previously been full-time mechanic, was now volunteering as deputy mechanic. He was a dab hand with the salvage pump, which could sometimes be tricky to start if you'd not used it much before. I was glad he was coming over with me.

When the *Ocean Way* came into sight at around eight o'clock, I sighed with relief. The coastguard helicopter *Rescue 900* was hovering above her and she was listing ever so slightly, but she didn't look too low in the water.

'Doesn't look like she's too heavily laden,' said Alan.

'I agree. It's a good sign,' I said.

But the adrenaline was still flowing.

Over the radio Ian Harms, our mechanic, confirmed our plan to *Ocean Way*'s skipper.

'We're sending two crew over with a salvage pump,' he said. 'We're coming alongside you now.'

The rest of the conversation faded from my earshot as I climbed out of the wheelhouse onto the deck, ready to board the *Ocean Way*. John appeared beside me with the salvage pump.

The trawler was still doing about nine knots, despite taking on water, so Alan had to keep pace alongside her. I could see three crew members gathering on the deck. I recognised two Latvian crew members, Roman and Vladimir, whom I'd worked with before, then spotted another familiar face.

Paul Moodie.

He was a fellow Orcadian – someone from Orkney – and in five months' time he was due to be best man at my wedding. I'd known him for nearly thirty years. I knew that he would be on board, and had him in mind as my first point of contact for a sitrep – an update on the current situation.

When the boats were close enough we passed the salvage pump over to the three men, then we climbed aboard. John went first, so he could set to work getting the pump running straight away, then I followed. Grabbing hold of the ladder that ran down the side of the trawler into the sea, we climbed up the side of the boat and then swung our legs over the railings at the top. As soon as my feet touched the deck, Roman and Vladimir grabbed my hand and shook it firmly. They were clearly glad to see a friendly face.

'Ah, Darren! You here to rescue us?' Vlad asked.

'Yeah, that's right, Vlad. Let's get this pump down below.'

Unlike other rescues, this time I had a clear picture of what to expect. I knew this boat like the back of my hand and I was pretty familiar with its crew too. As well as the skipper, Steven, Roman, Vladimir and Paul, there was an engineer called Ryan Mouat on board. Ryan was a local lad and this job was his first full-time foray into fishing. He'd only been crew for a year or so.

Once we'd got the pump down below and fired it up, I headed up to the wheelhouse to talk to Steven about transferring a couple of crew over to the lifeboat. After a brief chat, he declined.

'Skipper thinks it's better to have all hands on deck to help out,' I reported to John.

I understood his approach. On the surface everything seemed calm and under control. But I'd only been on the boat a few minutes when my confidence was replaced by concern. Looking around, the water was coming in much faster than I expected.

And much faster than the pump was churning it out.

I noticed a feeling in the pit of my stomach – a sickly, churning sensation. Even when John got the second pump going, it didn't seem to make a dent. The water just kept on rushing in.

John grabbed his VHF radio and spoke to the crew on the lifeboat.

'I think we're going to need another pump,' he said.

'We'll get one from the helicopter and come back alongside to pass it over,' Alan said.

'OK.'

Communications pinging back and forth, it was agreed that the lifeboat would receive a third salvage pump from the coastguard helicopter and then pass it to us on the trawler.

The chopper needed some wind resistance to push against, so it could drop the pump down, so the lifeboat pulled about a mile away to make the transfer, going head to wind. It would take a few minutes at least to sort.

As we waited, John and I continued to look for ways to stem the flow of water into the boat. Almost as suddenly as we started, I made a shocking discovery.

Water was flowing inside the boat through the scuppers!

The scuppers were flaps that washed water that had got onto the deck back out again. They were meant to be a no-return vent, a place for water to flow away – not come in.

Suddenly, adrenaline started to pump much faster round my body. Something was *seriously* wrong. When we'd arrived the boat hadn't looked all that low in the water.

But we'd only been on board a couple of minutes and the water was coming in through the scuppers. She was so heavy in the water they were practically submerged, with debris floating everywhere.

Was she starting to go down?

It wasn't just me that had noticed it.

Looking in at the volume of water rushing in, I took action immediately.

'Everyone stay on the upper deck,' I urged the crew. 'I don't want anyone down below apart from me.'

After that, I turned to John.

'Get the lifeboat on the VHF,' I said. 'Tell them we want to start transferring crew.'

Now, I just had to speak to the skipper.

Insist that we need to start preparing for the worst.

Confined to the wheelhouse, battling with the steering, and staying in constant communication with the coastguard and the lifeboat, he had his hands full and was still unaware of the gravity of the situation that was unfolding. After I calmly explained what was happening and made my recommendation, he reluctantly agreed to transfer Vlad and Roman to the lifeboat.

With the skipper on board with the plan, we swung into action. I went back down below to review the situation. Once again, it had worsened.

This time considerably.

There was now a couple of feet of water swilling around the deck at the deepest parts. It had started to lip over the stern hatch, down where the salvage pumps were situated.

I shook my head. This was it.

We'd reached the point of no return.

I returned to the wheelhouse to alert the skipper. He knew it was bad, but he was still convinced he could save the boat. After another discussion, we came to a compromise.

We'd get everyone else off, and I would stay aboard with him.

Together, we would continue to try to reach land.

Steven asked me to go down below to close the engine-room vents on the port side too. The *Ocean Way* had been fitted with brand new Caterpillar engines just a year earlier, and we wanted to see if we could save them. But when I went back below, it was obvious that it was now too late. The water on the port side was already up to the shelter deck.

The flaps were underwater.

Practically everything was underwater.

The boat was sinking – and fast!

It had all happened in the blink of an eye.

I bolted back up the steps.

'Right, we need to get everybody off!' I shouted. 'Now!'

There had already been a bit of fuss brewing.

The crew members that were going to transfer to the life-boat were scrambling around, grabbing rucksacks and passports. Now they were frantically pulling on the lifejackets that had been discarded earlier in the proceedings when they'd been running around trying to save the boat. The air was blue with expletives as the stress levels ramped up a notch.

Then I returned to the wheelhouse. This time there was no discussion. Only a statement.

'It's too far gone. We need to get off now,' I said.

Steven's face dropped, and I knew why. His world was quickly disappearing into an eerily calm and quiet sea.

It was the call that every skipper dreaded making.

Abandon ship.

But we had no other choice. As he went to his radio, I looked round at my colleagues. Concern shadowed their faces. I knew some of them weren't strong swimmers. I wanted to avoid anyone going in the water.

We were used to being at sea, not in it.

Taking a deep breath, I started herding the crew to the starboard side. Even though my heart was pounding in my chest, I had to keep my composure. These men, my friends and colleagues, were relying on us to get them home safely.

Funnily enough, it was something else we'd discussed many times as we'd worked through the night, coffee in hand. If the boat went down and we had to abandon ship, how would we do it?

In all the scenarios we'd concocted, we'd always had time.

Time to get into a life raft.

Time to wait to be transferred to a lifeboat.

Time to be winched into a helicopter.

But today, there was no time. If the lifeboat didn't reach us soon, we'd have to take the one option I wanted to avoid.

Jumping into the sea alongside an eighty-five-foot sinking trawler.

I could already feel the force of the water, pulling the *Ocean Way* deeper beneath the waves.

Just ahead, I had only moments ago watched as the helicopter dropped its hi-line into the sea. They had been planning to use it to transfer a third salvage pump to the lifeboat, which would in turn have transferred it to us on the *Ocean Way* before taking the fishermen onto the lifeboat. But I knew that plan would have been scrapped now.

They'd have heard the 'Abandon ship' call and would be on their way to assist us.

Now, Steven had stopped the engine. All we could hear was the sound of the chopper bearing down on us. At the same time, I could see the lifeboat powering towards us. They'd be with us any time now, so there was still a chance we'd be able to just step over.

Come on.

I heard the engine roar as the lifeboat came alongside us, then I heard a loud noise.

CLUNK.

The lifeboat seemed to ricochet off the side of the *Ocean Way* and we drifted apart from one another.

What the …?

I had no idea what had happened, but as well as the boat suddenly being too far away to cross from, the *Ocean Way* seemed to start being sucked down into the churning sea at an even faster rate. In that moment, I knew.

We couldn't wait any longer.

'We're going to have to jump in. Let the lifeboat pick us up,' I shouted. 'It won't be safe for us to jump across.'

At any rate, there wasn't time for Alan to bring the lifeboat back around.

The boat was already creaking and groaning, her nose in the air. Then, suddenly she began to slide even more rapidly underneath the waves, much, much faster than before.

She was about to go down!

What happened between the boat starting to capsize and me hitting the water was like a series of snapshots firing in my brain. It all happened so quickly. I knew the later we left it, the more likely we would be to get sucked down with the boat. We needed to jump as soon as we could.

And as far away as possible.

As we stood spaced apart on the starboard side, I think I must have shouted an instruction to that effect. Then I heard bodies hitting the water.

John, Roman, Vlad and Paul went first.

SPLASH. SPLASH. SPLASH. SPLASH.

At that point, I was furthest aft and the water was at my feet.

I was out of time.

I jumped, catching glimpses of Ryan and Steven in my peripheral vision, following quickly behind me.

SPLASH. SPLASH. SPLASH.

I felt my chest contract on impact with the icy cold sea. For a few seconds there was darkness and swirling confusion, to a soundtrack of the muffled rumbling of the boat being pulled down under behind me. Then I floated upwards and broke back through the surface of the water, gulping in huge mouthfuls of air. Scanning the water, I could see everyone starting to resurface, disperse and begin swimming at different angles towards the lifeboat.

I steadied myself immediately and looked around. Were any of the crew struggling? Did they need my help?

Yes.

I could see something towards the bow, and the deputy coxswain, Tommy Goudie, was pointing in that direction too.

It was the skipper.

He was about fifteen metres away from me, thrashing his arms around desperately, the creaking boat looming ominously in the background and a powerful swell dragging behind him.

He wasn't just struggling to swim. He was struggling to stay afloat.

Because he'd jumped in further along, he'd ended up closer to the boat, right under the flare of the bow.

Dangerously close to the suction that was dragging it down.

It must have only been 6°C in the water too. The temperature could easily have caused cold-water shock, and he'd be tiring quickly. All this on top of the fact that I knew he wasn't a strong swimmer.

If I didn't get to him, he'd be pulled down with his vessel. We'd probably never see him again.

Alive at least.

Mustering all the energy I possessed, I made a beeline for him. Crawling towards him, I pumped my arms as fast as they would take me, watching for floating debris as I went.

As soon as I got to him, I hooked my feet under his armpits and tried to use my arms to swim away.

Away from the Ocean Way. *And over to the lifeboat.*

My heart was racing. I could still feel the pull of the sinking vessel, tugging at us both and threatening to pull us under with it. But I kept swimming. Stroke after stroke, away from the boat, staying as calm as I could.

Eventually, I felt the pull weaken and I was able to drag us both clear of danger. Away from the crashing and swirling of the swell, I turned around in the water to see what had become of the rest of the *Ocean Way* crew and John.

I could see five figures bobbing around in front of me, all nearing the lifeboat. But as I looked, my stomach lurched. I couldn't make out who each one was, but a man was drifting towards the lifeboat's bow, while another was floating danger-ously close to its propellers.

Thankfully, Alan held the boat's position expertly, while the lifeboat crew leapt into action. If they hadn't, we might have had a tragedy on our hands.

Shouting instructions, casting boat hooks out to pull them in and preparing the A-frames – special manual hoists – on either side of the boat, they plucked the crew out of the water one by one.

They were almost all on board when I finally reached the lifeboat with the skipper. I secured him in the A-frame and called for him to be pulled up.

'Hold on tight,' I said.

'OK,' he gasped, still breathless and exhausted by his ordeal.

The lifeboat crew cranked him up by hand and hauled him

onboard. Once all of the *Ocean Way* crew were safe, John and I were hoisted up on the A-frame.

While my *Ocean Way* colleagues continued to watch the boat descend into its watery grave, I pressed on with my duties as RNLI crew. In twenty years of working at sea, I'd never seen a boat go down. Never.

And I never wanted to.

'She went quick,' said Alan, shaking his head.

If I'd been there as *Ocean Way* crew, I might have taken more time to ponder what I'd just seen. What it meant for my future. But I was there as RNLI lifeboat crew and my job wasn't done yet.

Once we'd got the *Ocean Way* crew some blankets and dry clothes to put on, we fished the rucksacks, boat hooks and life rafts back out of the water and secured them back on the lifeboat, before setting our course back to Lerwick.

When my work was done, I went to the wheelhouse and found my grab bag. Alongside my dry socks and other essentials, was a pack of cigarettes. I always kept a secret stash on the boat. I took them up to the deck and offered them around to the crew of the *Ocean Way*.

I think everyone had a cigarette that day, even the non-smokers.

Who could blame them?

As I looked around at their faces, shocked and sallow, it dawned on me. Every single one of us had just lost our job.

But at least we still had our lives.

The speed at which the *Ocean Way* went down, it could have been a very different story. Thinking of all the guys' families and friends, I got my phone out and opened my apps. By now, word would have got around that something serious was afoot.

I was Facebook friends with most of the crew's families, or at least someone who could get a message back. I imagined many of them would be in a state of panic. So I typed a quick status.

On way back. Everyone is OK.

I hit post and put my phone away. I hoped that simple note would put their minds at ease until we were home.

Forty-five minutes later, we were back at the station. Paramedics were waiting to check the *Ocean Way* crew over, while we prepared the lifeboat to go back into service.

Incredibly, everyone was fine. Only the skipper was showing signs of shock. His mother and father had turned up at the station when they'd heard what was happening. Before they left, I took his mother to one side.

'Get him showered and dried. Give him a Mars Bar and a bottle of Lucozade, and keep an eye on him,' I said.

'I will,' she said.

'He'll be fine,' I reassured her.

Ryan went home and Paul came back to mine, along with Roman and Vlad, who didn't have anywhere else to go. After a hot shower, a change of clothes and a hot drink, they all went on their way.

It had been quite a day for all of us.

The next morning, the whole fishing community knew about the fishing trawler that had gone down near Lerwick. It got picked up in local and national media, and there were reports from Australia, New Zealand, the US and Canada too.

Any time a fishing boat went down, the fishing community tended to find out, but with dramatic footage circulating of the vessel sinking, the *Ocean Way*'s fate seemed to have spread even further and wider than normal.

It was about four days before it hit me. Instead of being on the shout to rescue the *Ocean Way*, I could have been working on it.

Would things have been different if I had been?

There was no way of knowing. But I couldn't stop replaying the whole thing in my mind.

That memory of the vessel starting to slip faster and faster under the water.

It was haunting.

Despite knowing it was out there, I refused to watch the footage of the boat going down. What I remembered of being on board was quite enough. For a few weeks, the whole experience left me on edge. I'd jump at the sound of a loud bang at home, or twitch at an unfamiliar creak on the lifeboat. But in time, life returned to normal.

I set about finding new work straight away. The other *Ocean Way* guys did the same. Of course, I still volunteered with the RNLI. Seeing a boat that I worked on go down meant the importance of the service hit home even harder.

Time moved on. In August 2017, five months after the trawler went down, Gemma and I married, with Paul as one of my best men. Thankfully, he wasn't giving the speech, so our friends and family were spared hearing *Ocean Way*'s story all over again.

For a few months, I worked boat to boat, trying to find something more permanent. Something like I'd had on the *Ocean Way*. Eventually, something came along. But then there was news at the lifeboat station. Alan, the coxswain who had commanded the lifeboat on the *Ocean Way* shout, was planning to leave Shetland.

RNLI Lerwick needed a new coxswain. I started to consider it. I liked my new job, but I *loved* working on the lifeboats.

Why not make it my full-time career?

I couldn't see the harm in applying, so I did.

To my amazement, I got the job.

I've been the full-time coxswain at the RNLI's Lerwick Lifeboat Station for more than two years now. I've still never seen a boat go down and I can't even bring myself to watch the footage of the *Ocean Way* going down. It's not something I ever want to see.

It was a heart-breaking day for all of us crew, but I am glad that I was on call that day and able to help get my friends and colleagues to safety.

I never had any ambition or aim to take on a full-time RNLI role – I was more than happy just being a volunteer. But this job came along at just the right time. Working in this role, I see the care and support in our community more than ever. When I hear of a fishing boat broken down, I anticipate the pager going off – only to discover that another fishing boat is on their way to their location to tow them in.

5.

A LIFEGUARD'S HONOUR

Sophie Grant-Crookston, Perranporth 2006

I was working as a swimming pool lifeguard in Newquay in Cornwall when I heard that the RNLI was recruiting. It had just taken over managing the beach lifeguard service from the local council and it was making big changes. I enjoyed my job, but really I was an outdoors person and was going stir crazy working inside all day. So, when Greg Spray, my old swimming coach, told me about a lifeguarding job going on the south coast in Gyllyngvase, Falmouth, I jumped at the chance.

Even if I did prefer the waves of the north coast, over in Perranporth.

Everything changed when the RNLI took over. There was brand new training and fantastic equipment too. Out went the rickety old Land Rovers and in came shiny, powerful new trucks that went like a dream on the sand, as well as brand new boats and jet skis.

It was an exciting time to be starting my first ever beach lifeguard job.

With the RNLI came a culture shift too. At the time, life-guarding was a male-dominated profession. I'd come up through surf lifesaving club and even got my National Rescue Standards Beach Lifeguard Award. But despite having all the same skills as the boys, the idea of a girl getting into lifeguarding as a career wasn't usual. Not that I let that deter me. When I'd done work experience a year or so earlier, I'd told the one male lifeguard all about my ambitions.

'I'm going to apply to be a lifeguard after I finish school,' I said.

'It's a man's career, though,' he said.

I knew there was no rule against it. His was just an old-fashioned attitude.

Girls weren't strong enough.

I came up against it again and again.

'I keep getting told lifeguarding is a boy's job,' I said to my dad, Roy, one day.

'They think you can't do it because you're a girl?' he replied in his soft Glaswegian accent.

'Yeah,' I replied, shrugging in disbelief.

'Ach, you just get on with it,' he said, waving his hand.

That was my dad all over. Single-minded and no nonsense.

Well, I must have got it from somewhere.

By the time my work placement was over, I think I'd changed the opinion of male lifeguards – even if they didn't admit it. You see, I'd proved I was really capable. I could more than keep up with the boys I worked with. That was all the RNLI looked for. If you could meet its training standards, then you could do the job. Gender didn't come into it. Eventually a job came up at Perranporth and I found myself back on home turf, patrolling more challenging seas.

In peak season, there would be about eight lifeguards on Perranporth beach. Sitting elevated in the chairs on our RNLI trucks, you often couldn't even see the sand. There were just bodies, shoulder to shoulder on land, and a packed shoreline. It was gorgeous, but it could be dangerous. There were more than two miles of golden sands, and the waves attracted locals, holidaymakers and surfers – many of them beginners. But the waters were renowned for their strong currents and rip currents. It was such an interesting beach, with a real mix of people and challenges, that it even featured in a BBC TV series called *Seaside Rescue*.

For the most part, our job was about prevention. We'd provide information and mark out safe areas with ropes and flags, highlighting risks with signs screaming DANGER. We made it abundantly clear where people could swim, surf and play safely.

And where to avoid.

Providing the information was one thing. Getting people to listen was another. Most were respectful, only ending up in danger zones because they'd missed a sign or not heard our tannoy announcements. When we advised them to move, they usually listened to us. Others, however, thought they knew better. They'd saunter past huge warning signs and paddle off into a strong, rippy sea.

'You can't go in there,' I'd shout, running down.

'I've been swimming down here for twenty-five years,' they'd argue back.

'There's a rip current that could pull you out to sea,' I'd explain.

Sometimes they'd listen. Sometimes they wouldn't.

If they ignored our warnings, we'd log the conversation and hope they didn't get into difficulty. Often they wouldn't. But sometimes they would. When they did, the change in attitude was remarkable. They were all ears when you turned up on your surfboard to help them.

'Come on, let's get you back,' I'd say.

'Thank you. I'm really sorry,' they'd splutter, tails firmly between legs.

We never made a big deal of it, though. We weren't there to judge. Prevention was our goal, informing and advising people. But if they didn't take heed …

We were there to help. To save lives.

Every day on the beach was different. We'd find lost children, assist swimmers and surfers, and help people who'd stood on the weever fish that lurked in the shallows at low tide. In the summer we'd have *queues* of people waiting to dip their feet in troughs of hot water to relieve the bee-sting-like pain.

A lot of our work was routine. But not all of it.

Rip currents caused havoc on our beach. The sea could look clear and calm, but suddenly people paddling in the shallow waters would start to stumble and splash around, as if a rug had been pulled from beneath them. Because, in a way, it had. Rips were caused by the movement of the waves and its impact on the sand under the water. As the rip surged across the beach it would literally take the ground from under people's feet, causing them to suddenly find themselves out of their depth.

There were times when eight or nine of us lifeguards would find ourselves rescuing fifteen, thirty, even a hundred people, all at the same time.

Things really could shift from mundane to life-threatening in a heartbeat.

I might have only started working as a beach lifeguard in 2000, but I'd been a part of Perranporth's coastal community for as long as I could remember. My love of the water wasn't something that ran in the family, mind. My mum, Josie, was from Leicester and my dad was from Glasgow. Nowhere near the sea. But they'd made their home in Cornwall, so when I came along they wanted to make sure I stayed safe on the beach and in the water.

They enrolled me in the 'Nippers' class at surf lifesaving club when I was seven years old, first in Newquay and then over in Perranporth. I could swim before I could toddle and we learned beach skills from a young age. We covered everything from basic first aid and spotting rip currents, to treading water and lifesaving. It was so much fun. All the skills we learned just felt like a natural progression.

I'd spend evenings and weekends training with my mates, taking my lifesaving awards or travelling to surf lifesaving competitions all over the country. I couldn't get enough of it. By the time I was a teenager, Mum and Dad were a taxi service for surf lifesaving, ferrying us all over the place. I was lucky that their jobs, as a seamstress and electrician, gave them the flexibility to take me wherever I needed to be.

That said, when I was competing, I never wanted them to see me.

'Please don't come and watch,' I'd plead, my stomach in knots.

'OK, we won't,' they'd say.

But they always did. I'd catch them, hovering at the side lines, cheering me and my teammates on, just out of view so as not to put me off. In the end, I'd always be glad they showed up.

Their support never wavered. Not even when Dad had a life-changing car accident. I was thirteen when it happened. The crash itself was quite innocuous. Someone ran into the back of my dad's van. He wasn't badly hurt, but in the weeks that followed he developed unusual symptoms. Fatigue, tremors and stiffness. Eventually, after countless check-ups and tests, he had a diagnosis.

It was Parkinson's disease.

The crash had triggered the neurodegenerative condition, which causes you to lose nerve cells in your brain that produce dopamine. It affected his movement, but in many ways nothing much else changed. There were days when he couldn't get around as easily, but he never complained. The doctors gave him medication and he carried on working for a while, driving me to and from surf lifesaving and helping Mum around the house too. Dad's typically Scottish, no-nonsense attitude to his illness meant it never felt like a burden to anyone. Sometimes, if he was having a bad day, Mum would call me for help, and there were times when he'd end up in hospital, but that was about it. For the most part he just got on with things. We all did.

Time moved on. I got my job with the RNLI, something Dad was pleased as punch about. Eventually his symptoms did worsen and he had to give up his job. But he didn't give in to the disease. He kept himself busy. Whenever I got home from work, tea was on the table and he'd be there with a smile and a hug. If my car broke down and I was stuck somewhere, I'd call him and he'd be there. And if I forgot my sandwiches to take to work?

He'd bring them down to the beach for me, of course.

I was such a daddy's girl. Even when I met my boyfriend, Dave, a firefighter from Newquay, Dad was still my number one – and he knew it. When he started to find it harder to get around, and struggled to come and see me at the beach, I tried my best to go and see him every day and keep him updated on what I'd been up to.

'I always knew you'd prove the boys wrong,' he'd say, when we talked about my work.

'Well, you told me to get on with it,' I'd reply.

Six years into my career, I'd more than proved my point. There were already more girls following in my footsteps. I'd taken part in all kinds of rescues, trained in a host of new skills and learned how to use all of the equipment available to us, to ensure we could keep people on Perranporth beach as safe as possible. I'd even been brushing up on my rescue watercraft skills, using a special RNLI jet ski that had a rescue mat on the back. This craft was vital for getting out to casualties more quickly.

In fact, I'd been training on one of these with my colleague, Kris O'Neill, and some others one day in late September 2006. It was a glorious day, warm and sunny, but there was a strong surf coming in, making conditions out at sea choppy.

It was the type of day that could easily catch people out.

After the session, I'd come back to shore to grab some lunch and was just about to sit down, still in my wetsuit, when a call came into the station.

'There's someone stuck in the Bat Caves,' one of my colleagues said.

Apparently, a member of the public had seen a man stranded and called the coastguard, who in turn had contacted the RNLI. My ears pricked up. The Bat Caves – Bat Cave 1 and Bat Cave 2 respectively – were the local nicknames for a notoriously rocky gully at Droskyn Head, a dangerous corner of our patch. In fact, almost a year to the day, there had been a fatality in the same area. I didn't waste a moment.

'I'll go,' I said. 'Kris is out on the jet ski. Radio him and tell him I will run down. He can pick me up.'

'OK,' came the reply.

I burst out onto the sand and started running towards the water. In my peripheral vision I could see David Green, our senior lifeguard, waving Kris to return to land. Moments later he was bouncing back towards the shore, where I met him, jumped on the jet ski and lay down on the rescue mat.

'Someone's been seen in one of the Bat Caves,' I said.

'OK, let's go,' he said.

Neither of us knew what to expect when we got there. It sounded like the deceptively strong surf had taken someone by surprise, but we didn't know if they'd be in a fit state to swim or if they were injured.

What we did know was it would be rough. It always was around there.

The sea could be as placid as anything outside of that gully. But no matter what the conditions were like outside, on the inside the waves would be thrashing about, roaring each time one crashed on the rocks, creating a deafening echo. It was an assault on your senses. Apparently, the man had already been stuck there for a little while.

He must be terrified, I thought.

As we entered the gully, the sea was churning. Waves were lashing against the rocks and a huge swell was coming in. Up on the top of Droskyn Head we could see a crowd of people looking down, eyes wide with concern. I followed their gaze. Bingo!

I spotted him.

'There he is,' I shouted to Kris, pointing towards Bat Cave 2. A man in his thirties was stood propped up on a ledge alongside his surfboard, his face pale with fear. He'd managed to scramble out of the reach of the tips of the waves.

But he was still in real trouble.

I knew that things could go from mundane to life-threatening in a heartbeat.

If the swell picked up, which it could do at any moment, he could be swept off the rocks. If that happened, or if he decided to try to swim out himself, he'd never make it. He already looked exhausted. Even a few minutes trying to battle against the pull of the waves would drain the energy out of him.

He could get pulled under and drown.

As I scanned the gully to work out the best way to get to him, I couldn't help but think about the poor person who'd died in the Bat Caves a year earlier.

That's not going to happen today, I thought.

I could see straight away that it was too tight and rough to drive the jet ski right up to him. Kris noticed it too.

'I can't get us close enough,' he shouted over the waves.

'You're right. It's too dangerous,' I agreed.

'One of us will have to swim for him,' he said.

Time was of the essence. He was shaken and exhausted, and we needed to get to him as quickly as possible. If he ended up in the water, intentionally or not, one of us needed to be there to make sure he got out.

'I'll do it,' I volunteered.

Kris had his helmet and jet-ski kit on, while I was already in my wetsuit, ready to go. It made sense. Plus, if I wasn't confident, I wouldn't have offered. The man was about twenty-five metres away from us, the length of a standard swimming pool. The conditions made it challenging, but I'd grown up swimming in this surf. I'd trained in it. This was what we practised and practised for.

I've done it before, I can do it again now.

It was a huge test of all my skills.

Focused on my task, I tried to pull on my fins and rescue tube, a buoyancy aid that we used to bring people in. But the swell was tossing the jet ski around so violently that I was struggling.

'Oh God, I can't do this here,' I shouted to Kris over the crashing waves.

He didn't need telling twice. He pulled away and found a sheltered area of water just outside the cave, where I was able to slip on my fins, then he ran me back in, getting me as close as he could – about thirty metres from the man.

The plan was for me to swim out and get him, then bring him back to the jet ski, just outside the gully.

I climbed into the water and started swimming, my adrenaline pumping. I paid attention to the movement of the waves

– the swell was about six foot now. As the water ebbed and flowed, it would *woosh* into the gully and splash right up the sides of the Bat Cave, before pulling back out again. If I didn't time it right, I'd go a few metres forward, only to get pulled twice the distance back.

You can do this, I thought, focusing.

Nothing else went through my mind. I just did it.

Don't think, just do.

The waves hammered through the gully and I could feel the pull of the current. I fought against it as my arms made long, powerful strokes through the water, but as the waves retreated I got sucked backwards.

Try again.

I collected myself and waited for the wave behind me before I began swimming. This time, I made it a bit further. But not far enough. I got caught up in the swell once more, tossing me here, there and everywhere. As my whole head went underwater, blackness enveloped me and I could still hear the muffled roar of the waves, before I resurfaced to the crash of surf smashing against the rocks.

Come on, Sophie, I told myself.

As I started to regroup a second time, I looked around. Suddenly, my stomach lurched. Kris was nowhere to be seen.

Where had he gone?

I'd only been trying to reach the surfer for about five or ten minutes, but time seemed to dilate as I battled against the waves. My heart started to race, but I knew I had to keep my cool. If I panicked, Kris could be dealing with two casualties, not just one. I composed myself and looked over at the surfer, who was staring anxiously back at me.

I kept on going. Slowly but surely, I inched closer to the ledge, using every ounce of my strength to pull through the breaking waves and jagged pillars of rock. I could feel that I was cut and bruised from the sharp edges under the water, but eventually I made it.

Now all I had to do was climb up the rocks.

I surveyed the terrain and tried to work out a plan. Whichever way I looked at it, it was a difficult route to scramble up.

I'll try without my fins, I thought, pulling them off.

But just as I did, an almighty wave crashed into the cave and started to suck me backwards.

Not again! Gasping, I tried to steady myself in the water, struggling to pull my fins back on and swim against the pull of the waves.

It took a few attempts, but I finally found myself close enough to scramble up the rocks. As I pulled myself up over the ledge I found myself face to face with a very tired and scared young man.

'You're going to be OK,' I said calmly, as I checked the surfer over.

He'd been cut to shreds by the rocks.

He was shaking and bleeding a little, but he was all right. He'd be physically able to get in the water and swim with me. Glancing round, after about five minutes, I still couldn't see Kris. We'd been out of contact for about fifteen minutes now. With no jet ski to swim to, I had to formulate a new plan.

I had to get him out of there, jet ski or no jet ski.

I quickly attached the rescue tube to the surfer. I was going to have to swim him out of the gully alone. Once we were out and in calmer seas, he'd be in a much safer position. I began to prep him on what I planned to do.

This isn't going to be easy.

'We're going to jump in when the wave comes in,' I said. 'Make sure your back is to the wave, and if you need to hold your nose, do it.'

He nodded silently.

'After we jump in, I'm going to pull you really close to me,' I explained. 'We'll get through the next wave, then I'll swim.'

Another silent nod.

'You mustn't grab hold of me and pull me under,' I continued, knowing how people could panic. 'Just let me swim with you. I will keep you safe.'

'OK,' he said, reluctantly.

This was the thing with lifeguarding. Reaching the casualty was brilliant, but often it was only half the battle. You then had to get them back to safety, which could be difficult, especially if it meant swimming – even the shortest of distances – as there was a whole host of other dangers. Panic could be deadly if you couldn't keep the casualty calm, and there was always the chance that shock could set in as they hit the water.

You just had to make them trust you.

As we prepared, the man's face was clouded with fear, but the fact was, he had no choice *but* to trust me. I was his only way out of that cave. Ready to go, I started moving us into position, waiting for the wave. Then all of a sudden, I spotted something moving.

A flash of orange peeking out of the surf.

Holy Moly. It was our RNLI inshore rescue boat, a bright orange rigid inflatable vessel, bouncing across the waves. We used her to get to casualties stuck in the surf as quickly as we could.

'Hang on,' I told the surfer, raising my hand.

Change of plan.

I squinted towards the vessel. It was David. Another colleague, Robin Howell, was at the helm. David signalled to me, throwing his hand forward towards where we were perched. I knew what he was planning.

He was going to try to run the boat right into the gully.

I gave a thumbs-up, so they knew I was ready.

The boat had a much tighter turning circle than the jet ski, so it just might work. We watched as David waited for a lull in the waves. As soon as it came, Robin used the thirty-horse-power engine to roar into the gully, expertly turning into the oncoming swell and ending up with the ledge on his port side.

It was impeccable driving.

Made my task miles simpler too.

'Right. We need to jump in now,' I said to the man. 'Then I'll help you swim to the boat.'

'OK,' he agreed. He was still scared, but with a proper ride home in sight, it was easier to convince him.

'One, two, three …' I said.

The two of us jumped in. I could feel him near me as we plunged into the water. Once again there was darkness and muffled noise, then we resurfaced. As soon as our heads broke through the surface of the water, I grabbed him.

'Almost there,' I encouraged.

As we neared the boat, David and Robin were there waiting for us, arms outstretched.

'Thank you,' I said, as they hoiked us out of the water.

'You're welcome,' Robin grinned, then he turned tightly in the gully and powered out through the swell at top speed.

As we travelled back to shore, I learned what had happened while I'd been in the water. Kris had lost sight of me in the surf as I'd swum in. Concerned for my safety, he'd radioed for back-up and had to pull even further out of the caves.

With the only radio being on the jet ski, he'd had no way to communicate his plan to me, and just had to go for it. David had taken his call, and as he'd gone to launch the boat, he'd found Robin. He was off duty and about to go out for a surf. But when David asked him to take the helm, he'd dropped everything and they'd both set off.

And boy, was I glad they did.

It was typical of our little community. Everyone always pulled together.

You'd think we'd be exhausted when we returned to shore, but adrenaline's a funny thing. We were absolutely buzzing. As lifeguards, we never wanted to be faced with situations like this. But they happened – and when they did, there was no better feeling than getting someone back safely.

'Oh my God, oh my God,' I kept repeating, still absorbing what we'd done.

'That was such a good rescue,' said Kris, beaming.

'I had the easy end of the stick there,' said Robin. 'I had the engine. Sophie had to get in that water and swim.'

I knew it was an achievement and I was proud. I was proud of all of us.

There was no way I could have done it alone.

123

It was only when I got home to Mum and Dad's for my regular visit a few hours later that exhaustion finally came crashing down on me. I walked through the door and into the living room, then flopped onto the couch with a loud sigh.

'Busy day?' asked Dad, popping his head round the door.

'Not half,' I said. 'I had a massive rescue today.'

'You can tell us all about it over dinner,' he said.

Typical Dad, always ready with a slap-up meal and a listening ear. As we ate, I told them everything, still barely able to believe it had happened.

'You swam in the Bat Caves?' he gasped. 'No way!'

I wasn't surprised by his reaction. They were notorious.

'I did,' I said.

'You want to be careful doing that,' he said. 'But I'm proud of you.'

I smiled. He knew I was more than capable, but he was my dad. I was his little girl.

He was allowed to worry.

'Well done, Sophie,' Mum said.

Needless to say, once the adrenaline surge receded, I went home and slept like a log. In the days that followed, news of the rescue spread outside of Perranporth. Steve Instance, who headed up the RNLI lifeguards in our area, even came to the station for a debrief. He was really pleased with how it had all gone.

'Really well done,' he said. 'You did us proud.'

We knew our team had worked like the well-oiled machine we were meant to be. All alert, all working together safely and quickly. We even got a letter of recognition from Michael Vlasto, the operations director of the RNLI at the time, thanking us for our work and congratulating us on our success. The letter was signed off: 'I will see you very soon!'

I didn't think anything of it at the time, but I guess it was a hint of sorts, because shortly after the letter arrived, news came from RNLI's headquarters in Poole.

We were going to be formally recognised by the organisation.

Kris and David were going to be presented with service certificates, while Robin would be awarded the RNLI's Thanks of the Institution Inscribed on Vellum.

And me?

Honestly, I was stunned.

I was going to be awarded the Bronze Medal for Gallantry at the RNLI's Annual Presentation of Awards the following year. Medals were something lifeboat crews were always being awarded. It was much rarer for lifeguards to receive the honour. In fact, the first time a lifeguard had been awarded a medal was in 2003, just three years earlier. My friend from Newquay, Rod MacDonald, had been awarded it after rescuing a swimmer from a gully at Fistral beach. We'd all been so pleased for him.

Now I was getting one!

I was so overwhelmed, especially when I found out that the medal was the first one ever to be presented to a *female* lifeguard.

Not such a boy's world now, I thought.

That said, the rescue teamwork and bravery was from everyone involved. Without Kris, Robin and David's skills and quick thinking, my job would have been a heck of a lot harder. I was lucky to be a part of our big lifeguarding team.

A week after the rescue, we also learned that we'd won the Surf Lifesaving GB Rescue of the Year award. The whole escapade was still a hot topic of conversation when Mum and Dad came to have tea with me and Dave at our house in Newquay.

'I still can't believe you swam in those caves,' said Dad.

'I still can't believe I'm getting a medal,' I gasped.

'You deserve it,' he said with a smile.

We chatted happily all night as we tucked into the giant bowls of pasta and garlic bread that I'd prepared. Dad couldn't even finish it all.

'I'm stuffed,' he said, pushing his plate away. 'Thanks, Sophie.'

He did seem a bit quiet as he and Mum got up to leave, but I assumed he was just tired and full. The Parkinson's and his medication could sometimes drain him.

'Night, night. Love you,' I said as they left, giving them both a hug and a kiss at the door as we waved them off.

At six-thirty the next morning a noise shocked me awake. It wasn't my alarm clock. It was my phone, ringing. I picked it up and answered.

'Hello?' I croaked.

It was Mum.

'Sophie, you need to get over here,' she said. 'Your dad's not in a good way.'

It wasn't unusual for Mum to call. She'd done so countless times over the years. But this time it felt different. There was an urgency in her voice that I didn't recognise.

'I'm on my way,' I said.

I pulled on my clothes and jumped into the car. It took me minutes to make the five-mile journey to their house. I didn't even stop to speak to the doctor in the car that had pulled up outside; I just ran into the house and marched upstairs to my parents' bedroom.

What I saw stopped me in my tracks.

Dad was lying motionless on the bed with his head on the pillow. Mum was hunched over him, trying to give him breaths.

She was trying to resuscitate him.

For a split second, it was like everything stopped.

This was my dad. My hero and my world.

Despite his health struggles, he'd always been there for me. Just a few days ago he'd even come out to jump-start my car when I'd broken down.

Now he needed me.

I could either crumble or step up and help him.

Well, I knew what he'd do for me ...

Suddenly, something inside me clicked. I switched into life-saving mode. All my years of lifeguard training kicked in at once.

'Move out of the way, Mum,' I said.

God knows how I did it, but I managed to pull all sixteen stone of my dad off the bed, onto the floor and put him on his back. I tilted his head back and started to alternate between breaths and compression on his chest, trying to get his heart going. Over the years, I'd trained and trained for this, but only ever on a mannequin. Never a person.

I never imagined the first person I'd use this on would be my dad.

In the heat of the moment, that didn't even cross my mind.

I didn't think, I just did.

Just like I had during the rescue a few days earlier.

Moments after I started CPR, the doctor entered the room with a defibrillator.

I looked at him and spoke calmly.

'I'm a lifeguard,' I said. 'I can help you with this.'

He nodded and prepared the defibrillator.

I don't know how long we worked on Dad, me doing breaths and compressions, and the doctor using the defibrillator, but it felt like an eternity.

Eventually the doctor stopped and put his hand gently on my shoulder.

'I'm sorry, there's nothing there,' he said gently. 'We've got to stop.'

I knew he was right.

We'd done everything we could.

Everything was a blur after that. The paramedics turned up shortly after Dad passed. One was my friend Mike Gough, who knew me and Dave well from our work. He did everything he could to reassure me.

'You did everything right, Sophie,' he said. 'No one could have done any more than you did.'

I knew he was right, but it didn't stop me thinking.

Why couldn't it have worked? Why couldn't I save my dad?

The coroner came and arrangements were made. It was a heart-breaking time, but I had nothing but love and support from the RNLI and the rest of our community, who'd all known and loved my dad.

Receiving my Bronze Medal at the presentation in May 2007, eight months after the rescue and Dad's passing, was bitter-sweet. I was obviously proud and honoured, but it was hard not having him there to see it. He would have loved watching the rescue reconstruction on the huge screen in the Barbican in London, then seeing me go up on stage to receive the medal from the Duke of Kent. He might not have been there in body, but I knew he was there in spirit.

I had a huge support network around me. Mum was there, along with Dave, friends, relatives and managers from the RNLI. My dad's friend and my god-daddy, Billy Bell, even came all the way from Scotland to see it. I don't think I could have got through it without them all. I carried on lifeguarding until 2012, when I found out I was pregnant with my son Beau. Life changed a whole lot when he arrived in 2013. As much as I still loved it, lifeguarding just didn't fit in with our new routine. I started nannying for a local family and later got a job as a teaching assistant as well.

Despite the career change, I've stayed part of the lifeguard and coastal community, though. I'm always down the beach. Growing up around it, everything you learn sticks with you. You never lose it. I know if the RNLI lifeguards needed help one day, I'd just chip in. That's what we're like down here. You help as much as you can.

I'm still astounded that I'm in the RNLI history books as the first medal-winning female lifeguard, alongside so many other amazing female lifesavers. When I think of my twelve years as an RNLI lifeguard, I can recall so many different types of rescue that I was a part of, but that day in the Bat Caves is always at the forefront of my mind. The rescue only lasted about thirty minutes in total, but it was the biggest test of my skills and one of the greatest examples of teamwork that I had the honour of being part of.

Beau is six and a half now and he'll be starting 'Nippers' at surf lifesaving club soon. I'm doing exactly what Mum and Dad did with me. I want him to be safe at sea, but I also want him to have the experience I did – enjoying myself in a gorgeous environment with my friends. I want him to learn about being part of a community, learning to respect the water and looking out for one another. I hope he follows it as a career, because he'll have the best time. My years lifeguarding were the best years of my life. I'm really proud that I did my bit for paving the way for other girls wanting to get into the profession.

However, lifeguarding with the RNLI gave me something even more precious than all of that. It gave me the skills I needed to try to help my lovely dad when he needed me most. Because of the RNLI, I had the privilege of doing everything I could to try to save him. That to me is worth more than any medal or rescue in my entire career.

Although I'm not currently working with the RNLI, I see my career with it as on pause, rather than over. It's still with me, every day. I always see myself as an ambassador, and one day I'm determined to return as a volunteer, so I can give something back in return for everything the organisation gave to me.

6.

DRAMA AT THE BREAKWATER

Dave Riley, Eastbourne 2002

I'd recently left home and moved into my own place, but being twenty-three and living in rented accommodation, visiting your parents for a family meal was still a treat.

Not to mention a regular occurrence.

Tonight was no exception. It was blowing a gale and the rain was pounding down. I was looking forward to some home comforts after a busy day at work in Sovereign Harbour.

'Hello,' I called, as I walked through the door into the living room, then popped my car keys on the dining-room table.

My mum, Val, didn't miss a beat.

'Keys off the table, David,' she said, raising her eyebrow. 'We're about to lay the table.'

'But I need to know where they are,' I said. 'Just in case.'

I was volunteer crew with RNLI Eastbourne Lifeboat Station. If my pager went off, I liked to know exactly where my keys were so I could get on my way as quickly as possible.

Within minutes of arriving, the table was laid and Mum was just putting the finishing touches to the full roast dinner she'd been preparing. I sat down at my place and inhaled deeply. It smelled fantastic and I couldn't wait to tuck in. But just as she started to bring out the plates, the pager attached to my belt started to beep loudly.

BEEP BEEP, BEEP BEEP.

I leapt to my feet immediately and went to grab my keys from where I'd put them on the table. But they were gone.

'Where are my keys? Where are my keys?' I asked, quickly scanning all around. I looked over at my dad, Bernard. I knew he'd set the table.

'Where have you put them?' I asked.

'Let's have a look,' he said.

Eager to get on my way, I started shuffling through newspapers on the sideboard. Mum and Dad started looking too, until I eventually heard a jangling sound beneath a pile of papers that I'd been rummaging through.

'Got them,' I announced. 'I'm off!'

'Take care, David,' Mum said. She supported my work with the RNLI, but she always worried about me.

'I will,' I said. Then I turned to Dad. 'Are you coming down?'

Dad wasn't a crew member, but he had an interest in the lifeboats and the sea. Back when I was a kid, the lifeboat crew were called by the maroons. It was an iconic sound. Two loud rockets were fired to alert them to the fact that someone was in distress. When Dad and I used to hear them go off, we'd jump in the car together and rush down to the seafront to watch the old Rother class lifeboat launch down the slipway.

I could still recall the excitement.

But now our roles had reversed. If I was with him when my pager went off, I always asked him if he wanted to come along.

Mark Criddle, coxswain at RNLI Torbay Lifeboat Station.

The 6,395-gross-tonne vessel the *Ice Prince* seen sinking in the English Channel after its crew's dramatic rescue in 2008.

Coxswain Mark Criddle's enduring memory of the rescue, from the flying bridge of the Severn class all-weather lifeboat, the *Alec and Christina Dykes*: 'Pulling up towards the ship to see my crew with their arms outstretched . . . risking everything to grab hold of a complete stranger.' (Photo taken during reconstruction.)

Islay's Severn class lifeboat,
Helmut Schroder of Dunlossit II.

Islay coxswain David MacLellan, who
led a crew of five to rescue a stricken
yacht and its lone skipper from the
treacherous reef of Skerryvore.

Mark Taylor-Gregg, who took part in the furthest English shout
on record for the RNLI – 110 nautical miles – during his first stint
as navigator at Tynemouth in 2015.

In 2017 RNLI volunteer crew member Darren Harcus found himself called to the assistance of the *Ocean Way*, a vessel on which he'd worked for five years. His soon-to-be best man was one of the crew he helped to rescue.

The view from the wheelhouse of the *Michael and Jane Vernon*, Lerwick's Severn class all-weather lifeboat, during a training exercise.

Beach lifeguards Kris O'Neill and Sophie Grant-Crookston power out towards Perranporth's infamous Bat Caves on an RNLI rescue watercraft (RWC) in a reconstruction of their dramatic rescue of a stranded surfer.

Sophie Grant-Crookston, the RNLI's first ever medal-winning female lifeguard.

Crew member Dave Riley as a fourteen-year-old boy, with Eastbourne's Rother class lifeboat the *Duke of Kent* in 1993.

RNLI Eastbourne's crew on the breakwater at Sovereign Harbour in full all-weather kit, following a dramatic service to the sinking yacht *Paperchase*. Pictured from left to right are Dan Guy, Dave Riley, Mark Sawyer, Richard Welch, Ben Delaunay (sitting) and Keith Murphy. Coxswain Mark Sawyer received a Silver Medal for Gallantry and mechanic Dan Guy was awarded a Bronze Medal for Gallantry for the 2002 rescue.

Opening the boat shed in preparation for the launch of
Exmouth's D class lifeboat, *George Bearman I.*

Exmouth RNLI's Roger Jackson, who returned to the service after
a horrific paragliding accident in 2001 that almost cost him his legs.
His courageous actions on a shout ten years later saved four lives
and earned him a Bronze Medal for Gallantry.

'I felt the strength draining out of me, slipping away like sand in an egg timer.'
RNLI Portrush mechanic Anthony Chambers reflects on fighting against
a rising tide to rescue two young boys from a cave.

Aileen Jones, RNLI Porthcawl's first
female helm, with her Bronze Medal
for Gallantry.

Porthcawl Lifeboat Station's tractor,
which was used to launch its Atlantic
75 class lifeboat *Giles* for the 2004
rescue of the *Gower Pride*.

At just twenty-four years old, Castletownbere coxswain Dean Hegarty faced the challenge of his career when a mayday call came in.

'If vessels got into trouble near the Piper's Rocks, they needed help in minutes, not hours.' Dean Hegarty's local knowledge meant he understood his adversary on the night of the 2018 rescue.

Inside the wheelhouse of RNLI Castletownbere's three-million-euro Severn class lifeboat, the *Annette Hutton*, during a night-training exercise.

Chapel Porth beach in St Agnes – the location of many a significant moment for Vicky Murphy and her family, not least when she and her partner Marc were dramatically rescued in 2009. Vicky was heavily pregnant with her daughter Rae at the time of the rescue.

Vicky Murphy and her daughter Rae on Chapel Porth beach, ten years on from their rescue. Rae still treasures the teddy bear gifted to her by Chris Lowry and Damian Prisk, the RNLI lifeguards who saved their lives.

Tonight, though, he wasn't that keen.

'Oh no, your mum's just served up,' he said. 'I won't come tonight.'

I couldn't blame him. It was cold and dark, and the rain was lashing down.

There probably wouldn't be much to see, I thought.

In these conditions it was going to be a really miserable shout, whatever it was I was heading out to. But that didn't stop me.

I jumped into my car and four minutes later I was at the lifeboat station. I parked up, ran across the lock gates at the marina and burst through the doors. Quite a few volunteers were already there, and the coxswain, Mark Sawyer, was bringing everyone up to speed.

'Right, we've got a yacht outside,' he said. 'Its crew was holding off in poor weather.'

It wasn't uncommon for this to happen. Usually, we'd go out to assist, then stand by to escort them into Sovereign Harbour when it was safe to do so. But tonight was different.

The yacht was a Sigma 33 Bermudan sloop called *Paperchase*. It was on its maiden passage under new ownership from Ramsgate to Eastbourne. There were believed to be just two crew on board, the skipper and his female partner. While en route, the yacht had started experiencing severe weather about three nautical miles east of the harbour. The skipper had contacted the harbour's duty officer, Jason Foster, and stated his intention to enter.

But with a Force 8 wind blowing in from the south-east, the conditions were the worst they could possibly be for entry into Eastbourne. There was shoal water – an area of water shallower than the surrounding water – to the east and west, and the exposed wreck of the SS *Barnhill* midway along the channel. The way was littered with risks.

Jason had advised them to hold off, but the yacht had continued its approach.

After that, the inevitable had happened.

'They've gone aground just outside the harbour,' Mark continued.

I shuddered. Working at the harbour and knowing the wind conditions, that wasn't good at all. The strong south-easterly winds would be blowing the vessel right towards the harbour entrance – two big piers made of large granite rocks. As well as being miserable, it was going to be shallow and nasty out there tonight.

The coxswain started selecting his crew.

'Benjamin Delaunay, Keith Murphy, Mark Osborn,' he said. 'Daniel Guy, Richard Welch and David Riley.'

My ears pricked at hearing my name.

I was up.

I moved through to the changing area as we all pulled on our yellows – our personal RNLI yellow kit. Looking at the crew Mark had selected, I could tell he was anticipating a tricky night. Benjamin, Keith and Mark were in their late forties and had plenty of experience between them. The rest of us, despite being younger, had worked on the lifeboats for a long time. In fact, Dan and I had both joined the crew at around the same time, when we were seventeen.

We'd come up through the ranks together and now he was the full-time mechanic, while I was usually allocated as the navigator or radio operator. As we launched from the station and powered towards the yacht, I took my place at the chart table, with the coxswain at the upper steering position. Ahead I could see foamy waves creeping to about three metres in height. The coxswain turned to me.

'Dave, I need you to stay down below on the radio tonight,' he said. 'And we need to keep the door shut as much as possible.'

'OK, no problem,' I said.

Instinctively, I turned around to check that the wheelhouse door of our all-weather lifeboat was closed tightly. Keeping the door shut wasn't the norm. We only did it if there was a high chance that water was going to get in. If that happened, it could upset the stability of the boat.

If the coxswain was asking for a closed door at this point, it could only mean one thing.

It was going to get rough.

And quickly.

I'd always known I wanted to join the RNLI. At the age of ten, when all my friends were imagining being police officers and firefighters, I was dreaming of being out on the lifeboats. Despite my enthusiasm for jumping in the car with Dad when the maroons went off, I think my parents thought I'd grow out of it. But I didn't.

The lifeboats took precedence over everything when I was a teenager. If the maroons went up while I was doing my paper round, I'd sling the newspapers back into the garage, and go to watch the lifeboat launch. I'd only continue my round after the boat and its crew were completely out of sight.

If my employers had ever found out …

As far as I was concerned, the closer I was to the lifeboats the better. So when I turned sixteen and was faced with the choice of going to college to do media studies or take a job at Sovereign Harbour as a YTS trainee, it was a no-brainer.

Although I'd always been interested in the media and had good enough qualifications to go to college, the marina was next door to the lifeboats.

Once I'd made my choice, I took advantage of my proximity to the lifeboat station. I quickly got to know the coxswain, Dave Corke, and made sure I expressed my enthusiasm for the RNLI.

You had to be seventeen to enrol, but I figured that if they already knew me, I'd be able to get in quicker. My approach worked. Dave allowed me to fill in all my paperwork straight away, so that as soon as I turned seventeen I was enrolled. On my seventeenth birthday, I received the best present ever.

My RNLI pager.

But because I was under eighteen, I needed parental consent before I could go anywhere near the lifeboats. I took the form to my mum immediately.

'I need to you to sign this, so I can join the RNLI,' I said.

'Better drowned than duffers if not duffers won't drown,' she said as she signed the form.

'What does that mean?' I asked. Mum just smiled.

'You'll learn,' she said.

I didn't realise it at the time, but it was a line from the famous Arthur Ransome novel, *Swallows and Amazons*. In the story the children had written to their father, who was away with the navy, to ask permission to sail the *Swallow* to an island

and camp out alone. He'd replied by telegram with the same line my mum did. Once I'd read the book, I understood.

She was telling me to go for it, but to be careful.

For the first three months of my enrolment I remained on shore, learning about the station and how it worked. RNLI Eastbourne's set-up was a bit different to others across the country. We had an all-weather lifeboat based in the marina, and two miles down the road, where Dad and I used to watch the old Rother class launch from, was the inshore lifeboat station.

At first I helped on the beach with the inshore lifeboat, shovelling the stones after storms, washing and fuelling the boat, and making sure she was always ready to go. It was the real nitty-gritty work that most people didn't want to do. But I did it. Looking back now, it was a test. Before making me lifeboat crew, the coxswain wanted to be sure.

Can he get stuck in?

Can he do the stuff that nobody enjoys doing?

Will he keep coming back?

Well, I stuck it out. After three months I had my medical, and I was then invited onto boat training. Around the same time another lad of my age joined the crew.

His name was Daniel Guy. With both of us being seventeen and vying for a place on the boat, there could have been real rivalry, but that wasn't how the RNLI worked and it wasn't how we were. Instead, we built a good working relationship. For six months we went out on all kinds of exercises together, rough-weather training – the lot. We both always turned up, despite knowing we probably wouldn't get picked for the shout. Certainly not together.

Two newbies together could be a real liability.

Both of us understood that we had to wait our turn, and we were happy enough to stay behind and do our bit on shore.

Until it was our time.

Then one day it happened. It was a really rough day and the pager had gone off. I turned up as usual, driven to the station by my dad, as I hadn't yet passed my driving test. I was one of the first there, and, as a life was in danger, the helm, Gary Mead, was quick to pick his crew for the inshore lifeboat.

Suddenly, he was looking directly at me.

'You,' he said, pointing.

Stunned, my jaw swung open. I looked over my shoulder to see if there was someone behind me. When I saw there wasn't, I pointed at myself. For a moment it felt like I was the only person in the room.

Was it my turn?

'Me?' I asked. 'You want me to come?'

'Yes,' he said. 'Get kitted up.'

Turns out it *was* my moment.

My first shout.

I'm sure there were some words running through my head but I can't remember what they were. My heart was racing. There was a windsurfer in difficulty, down in a place called Normans Bay, and they needed our assistance. The two other crew that the helm had picked were really experienced, so I felt honoured. The launch was rough, but I don't remember being scared, just driven by adrenaline and focused on the job that needed doing.

The all-weather lifeboat launched from Sovereign Harbour and escorted us through the rough seas. It took us about twenty minutes to go two miles as the weather was so bad, tossing us around like a bath toy, rain and sea spray battering us as we went.

In the end, though, it was reported that the windsurfer had managed to get themselves ashore to safety, so we were stood down.

The all-weather lifeboat was instructed to escort us back in, but as we dropped into the trough of each wave, we'd lose sight of everything, even the big lifeboat. In the end we beached. Safely – but still.

As first shouts went, it was a baptism of fire.

And I'd loved it.

The next day, my pager went off again. This time I knew there was a chance I'd be picked, so I was even more eager than usual to get to the station. I'd been out once now, after all. When I walked in I was met by smiles from the older crew members.

'So, you've come back then, Dave?' Gary said.

'Why wouldn't I?' I said.

Gary turned to Dave Needham, another helm who had been out with us the previous night.

'Right, we haven't scared him off,' he laughed. 'He's going to be with us for a while.'

I didn't intend it to be any other way.

I'd been well and truly bitten by the bug.

After three months on the inshore lifeboat, I was invited up to join the all-weather lifeboat crew as well. The more I turned up, the more experience I gained. I worked in the marina five days a week. Sundays and Mondays were my days off, but I soon began spending my days off at the lifeboat too.

'Monday is cleaning day,' Dave Corke, the all-weather lifeboat coxswain, said to me one day.

'On the lifeboat?' I asked.

'Yes,' he replied. 'You've got every Monday off work. If you come and help me with an hour's cleaning, I'll spend an hour with you doing a bit of chart work.'

Dave took great pride in keeping the all-weather lifeboat ship-shape.

'OK,' I said.

It seemed like a fair deal.

For me, it was another opportunity to learn. I'd turn up every Monday to polish the brass and clean the lifeboat from top to bottom. Once the boat was gleaming, Dave would sit down with me and teach me how to plot positions and work out search patterns, and other navigation skills.

I soaked it all up. Unlike other teenagers, I wasn't interested in going out drinking. Drinking would mean I couldn't go out on a shout if one came in. My social life revolved around the station, its crew and learning as much as I could from more experienced staff and volunteers.

I turned up and turned up. Until one day I didn't.

I'd driven over to Brighton to visit my girlfriend. Back then there was no online availability system that allowed us to share when we'd be on call, and, being young, I hadn't remembered to mention I was going away. When I returned the next day, the coxswain called.

'I waited for you. Where were you?' he asked.

'Err, I was in Brighton,' I said. 'Visiting my girlfriend.'

My stomach was churning with nerves. I'd never been told off by him before.

'I could have done with you on the chart table,' he said. 'And you didn't turn up.'

'I'm sorry,' I said.

But in that moment, I realised. He wasn't telling me off. He was letting me know something. I wasn't just some young volunteer learning the ropes anymore. I was competent.

I was relied upon.

It was a special, if scary, moment for me. One that never left me. From then on, my pager never left my side.

By the age of twenty-one I was a helm on the inshore lifeboat – quite a young age to reach that position – as well as crew on the all-weather lifeboat. Being able to work both boats was great, but it meant I was faced with a choice whenever the pager went off.

At the bottom of my road, each time, I'd have to decide.

Left or right?

Inshore or all-weather?

I began to gravitate towards the all-weather boat. The station was closer to where I lived, so I could get there much more quickly. In time I became one of the main navigators on board, a role that often doubled up as radio operator. After all those cleaning days on the boat with Dave, I was fluent in my chart work, but there was another reason that I assumed this position.

I didn't suffer with seasickness.

On a rough night some of the crew couldn't bear to be down below, let alone looking down and reading a chart. It was a gift that not everyone had and one that I'd be grateful for throughout my career.

At half past six in the evening, around four minutes after launching, we were pushing outside the harbour towards the *Paperchase*. As we bounced up and down, up and down, on the crests of three-metre-high waves, I was once again grateful for the strong constitution that had earned me my seat on the lifeboat.

The sea's rhythm was relentless.

With one eye on my charts, I made contact with Dover Coastguard to give them our crew list, while they confirmed our task to us.

'Eastbourne Lifeboat, this is Dover Coastguard. You are launched to a thirty-three-foot yacht who has made an approach to Sovereign Harbour and is now being blown onto shallow ground and buffeted by waves,' the coastguard said.

'Roger. All received,' I said. 'Will call once we have more information.'

Next, I tried to call the yacht to inform them of our approach.

'*Paperchase*, this is Eastbourne Lifeboat,' I said. Then I waited for a response. But nothing came back.

'*Paperchase*, this is Eastbourne Lifeboat,' I tried again.

Still nothing. A knot tightened in my stomach.

What are these people going through? I thought.

All the possible scenarios spun through my head.

Was the radio on? Was it off? Were they down below? Or up on deck? Had they been washed overboard?

'Why are they not talking to me?' I said aloud.

It took us five minutes to reach the scene. As we left the safety of the breakwater, we began to feel the full force of the weather. Waves were crashing over the bow and the lifeboat was taking on a considerable amount of water.

Exactly why the coxswain had wanted the door closed, I thought.

It was pitch dark. With no moon or ambient light to guide us, we relied on the glare of our searchlight to illuminate the scene.

Up ahead, the yacht slowly came into view. I gasped slightly. The headsail was still up and the boat was beam on to sea, tilted on her side and being battered by waves. Every time one collided with the vessel it would come right up, then land, crashing over her.

It appeared that, as the crew had tried to make their entrance, the yacht had been hit by a wave that had pushed them offshore. They must have attempted to come back around into the channel, then been hit by another wave and ended up completely out of control. They'd run aground less than one hundred metres from the northern breakwater.

Despite this, it was still too far from shore for them to step off the boat and wade to safety. If they had done that, they'd have been completely out of their depth. In this weather they'd have probably been swept away and ended up washed ashore somewhere.

Who knows if they'd have survived that or not?

Searchlights on, we continued powering towards the stricken vessel. Despite the rain and spray coming in towards us, I could see a figure moving on board, near to the mast. I briefly opened the door to call up to Mark.

'What's that?' I asked.

'Must be one of the crew,' Mark said.

I looked more closely, as our searchlight lit up the deck. I couldn't make out if it was a man or a woman, but whoever it was, they were clinging on to the mast for dear life, helpless to do anything else.

'I'm going to back in towards them,' said Mark.

'OK,' I said.

'Update the coastguard and request shore assistance,' he said.

I got on the radio immediately. If either of the crew were washed ashore, they'd need help urgently. And if the lifeboat foundered?

We'd need help too.

Mark had no choice but to keep the boat facing into the sea. If we just drove in towards the *Paperchase*, there was every chance that we would be caught side on and knocked clean over.

As we backed in, the boat was being tossed up and down on each wave. All of our instruments and the echo-sounder were flashing. The breaking waves meant there was too much air under the boat, so the instrument couldn't get a signal.

I had no idea what depth of water we were actually in.

The only time I could tell was when I felt the hull of the lifeboat bumping the bottom, hitting the ground beneath the waves.

CLUNK. CLUNK.

As we made contact, the echo-sounder seemed to flash faster and more urgently, until the next wave bounced us up again. At any given moment there was no more than half a metre between the hull and the seabed.

Our Mersey class was designed to deal with conditions like this. Its propellers were protected, so we knew we could take a little bit of contact. But it was a fine line. And if we ran aground ourselves, we'd be no good to anybody.

If we were to get close enough to the *Paperchase* to pass a line over, we needed to stay calm and work carefully. With a line on the yacht, the crew would be able tie it to the bow and we'd be able to tow them to safety.

Slowly, Mark manoeuvred the lifeboat towards the vessel, until we were about ten metres away, bumping the bottom all too frequently, as the troughs of the waves came through. Mark stopped backing in.

'I can't get in any closer,' he said.

We were still too far away to pass a line over, and, with the winds still blowing a gale, it was too dangerous for us to stay in that location.

We couldn't risk our own crew and lifeboat.

In a flash, Mark started moving back out, pulling us about thirty metres away from the yacht. In deeper water, but still facing the sea and being thrashed by breaking waves, we had to formulate a new plan.

For a moment, he assessed the scene in front of him. Then he spoke.

'Let's try heaving a line across. We can use it as a messenger line. Dan, will you take charge?'

'OK,' Dan said.

If Dan was able to get the line over, we could attach a tow rope to the line for the *Paperchase* crew to then haul across and attach to the bow.

It might just work ..., I thought.

Mark once again skilfully manoeuvred the lifeboat, head to sea, towards the yacht as I continued to radio the vessel. We knew there were at least two people on board, but there could be more.

I had to keep trying to make contact.

At that moment, we were going in on a wing and a prayer, hoping the crew member on deck would know what to do with the line. If I could get hold of someone, I could provide proper instructions and find out what was going on over there.

I watched through the back window as Dan raised his arm and tossed the line towards the man on the deck of the *Paperchase*. No doubt one of the other guys was shouting instructions through the loudhailer as well, but with our doors closed I couldn't hear. All I could do was watch.

I saw the line fly into the air, only to be snatched away by the wind. My heart sank, but undeterred, Dan made a second attempt. Once more, the lightweight line was torn from its intended path. Then he tried again and again, but to no avail. Within metres of the yacht, its headsail now shredded and whipping dangerously about in the wind, our lifeboat also remained in a precarious position.

After Dan's fourth attempt, I could tell that Mark was concerned about our position, so he made a judgement call. Mark called over the intercom from the upper steering position.

'This is too risky. I'm pulling us away.'

Then he added, 'We're going to need the rocket lines.'

In my six years on crew, we'd never used the rocket lines while out on a shout. A rocket line was the size of a regular bucket, the kind you'd take out to wash your car. Down the centre of it was a rocket, not dissimilar to a firework, with a 150-metre length of twine attached, about the thickness of a shoelace.

You could attach the end to your main tow line and – in theory – fire the tow line right over the destination boat, giving the crew a better chance of grabbing hold of it. We'd practised with the rockets before, out in open sea, but using them in anger?

This was a first.

We pulled away again. With the sea still tossing us about violently, we leapt into action as best we could, but I was still being rattled about inside the wheelhouse. I went to the flare locker, threw open the door and grabbed two white flares, which would be used to illuminate the deck once the boat was under tow. Then I went to grab the rocket lines.

'We're going to fire the first one and see where it lands with the winds,' said Mark. 'Hopefully, with that knowledge, we'll get it right on the second one. It'll go over the yacht and they'll be able to grab it.'

I took a deep breath. We were aiming from about fifty metres away, into a storm that was blowing a hooley. Were we going to get it through?

We'd better hope so.

You see, there were only two rocket lines on the boat. Our two chances to get a tow over to the *Paperchase*.

I prepared the first rocket line and sent it up to Dan, whom Mark had tasked with firing it. At the same time the rest of the crew brought the tow out of its locker and attached it to the rocket line.

As Dan prepared to fire the test shot, you could cut the tension on deck with a knife. I was already preparing the second rocket line. The mood on the boat was frenetic, and after Dan fired the line the pace would ramp up again. Once we knew where the line had landed, we'd need to get the second one fired pretty quickly, before the conditions changed again.

Everything was shifting, second by second.

Just before we closed the door to the wheelhouse to prevent too much water getting in, I could hear a voice booming out instructions through the loudhailer.

'When the line lands across the boat, get hold of it and pull.'

Once again, I watched as Dan raised the rocket line and fired it towards the yacht. Unlike the heaving line we'd tried earlier, this was heavier and had more force behind it. It stayed on course, flying through the sea and spray …

I held my breath.

Where would it land?

Watching intently, hoping for the best, we soon had our answer. It glided straight over the yacht and landed on the other side.

No way! I thought.

'He's done it!' Mark exclaimed.

I was left relieved – and surprised too. I couldn't believe my eyes. The first time we'd ever used the rocket line in active service, and he'd only gone and done it in one.

In these conditions too!

Stunned by what I'd just seen, I was taken by surprise as a wave rolled in and jolted the lifeboat. I took a half-step back to steady myself, but as I did, I kicked the door of the flare locker and fell backwards into the boat.

'Woah!' I shouted, as I went.

Truth be told, I was a little shaken. Everything was moving at a frantic pace. I steadied myself and took a deep breath, before I returned the second rocket line to its storage.

Hopefully, we wouldn't be needing it again tonight.

Through the back window, I could see that the casualty who had been clinging onto the mast was a man, the boat's skipper. Not far away from him was his female shipmate.

At least it explained why no one was responding on the radio.

Eventually, the white flares went up and illuminated the area. Goodness knows how, but Dan and the crew on deck convinced the skipper to let go of the mast and shuffle forward to grab the tow rope that had landed across his deck.

He was wet, frightened and probably already exhausted, but with a combination of waving, shouting and sheer hoping, they encouraged him to secure the tow rope to the bow of the *Paperchase*. All the while, Mark held our position. Even as we were being battered by the wind and the waves, his skill ensured that the boat didn't move and the line wasn't snatched from the skipper's hands.

It was seamanship at its finest.

Once we were firmly attached to the yacht, we let out some more line, enabling us to move into deeper, safer water and out of the path of the breaking waves that were throwing us around. As we did, the front of the yacht started to pull round too, re-floating again, just as we'd hoped.

Finally, we were all able to let out a little sigh of relief. The tension on board dissipated slightly and after we'd towed the yacht about fifty metres along, my VHF radio crackled into life.

It was the skipper of the *Paperchase*.

'We're on tow,' he said. 'We're coming away.'

'How many on board?' I asked.

'Two crew. All safe and well.'

'How is your vessel?'

'All is well on board.'

I heaved an even bigger sigh of relief. With the black hole of radio silence filled, we could communicate properly to orchestrate the rescue of crew and vessel once we were in deeper waters.

Brilliant. We've got this now.

I opened the door to relay the communications to Mark. But almost as soon as I had, I heard Dan speak, concern rising in his voice.

'Hang on. Is she listing?' he asked. 'Has she got a lean on?'

I turned to look through the back door. Someone had opened it as soon as we'd moved out of the big breaking waves. I tilted my head slightly, then sucked in a deep breath. He was right.

She was listing!

We barely had a moment to contemplate what might be causing the list, when suddenly the lifeboat pitched violently. A series of large waves had suddenly rolled in against us, knocking us sideways. As the wave train continued, it rolled straight into the *Paperchase*. She tipped onto her side and her crew were washed overboard.

In less than a minute, the *Paperchase* had gone from re-floating and being towed to keeling over onto her starboard side, mast in the water. Moments later she was starting to sink, bow first. Our momentary relief was over in a heartbeat.

The situation had gone from bad to the worst it could possibly be.

Now wasn't the time to panic. Time was running out and we had to assess the situation. We were now attached to a sinking yacht, close to the shallows of the breakwater and we had two exhausted people in the water, bobbing around among dangerous debris.

I called the coastguard immediately.

'Dover Coastguard, this is Eastbourne Lifeboat, *Paperchase* has capsized and we have two people in the water.'

'All received,' came the coastguard's reply.

Mark reacted immediately, easing up the lifeboat as the crew sprang into action, cutting the tow and releasing the yacht. Next they pulled the line up, so we didn't get it tangled in our propellers. The yacht was now drifting, submerged in the water. By the time we came back around, it was clear the vessel was beyond recovery. Our mission was now to rescue the two crew from the turbulent water.

There were ropes, sails and sail covers floating all around the capsized yacht, with only a portion of her port side now visible above the water. Among all this, in the pitch dark, were two people, clinging onto the submerged rails on the side of the yacht.

It was a relief to see they were both still OK.

But how were we going to get to them?

'We can't drive the lifeboat alongside this,' I said, thinking aloud.

'We'll get in as close as we can and throw heaving lines out to them,' Mark said.

The crew on deck started a production line, snaking the rope up onto the deck as Mark brought the lifeboat in as close to the vessel as he could. Once we were at our safe limits, the deck crew launched the heaving line into the water towards the two casualties.

Twice the line was washed away by breaking waves, but on the third attempt we managed to get close in, within four metres of the casualty vessel and its crew. With Mark holding our position skilfully, the guys managed to pass the heaving line and the tow line over to the female crew member of the *Paperchase*.

Yes! I thought.

Somehow, she managed to wind the ropes around both of them, holding on tightly to the rope and the skipper. Even from my position in the wheelhouse, I could see he wasn't in a good way.

With help from the crew hauling her towards us, she ended up a little forward of the lifeboat. Now she had no choice but to let go of the skipper. She hesitated for a moment, then released her grip. As she did, Benjamin, Keith, Mark Osborn and Richard pulled her towards the port shoulder of the boat. Without his partner holding him up, the skipper looked limp and like he was already starting to slip under the water.

Fighting the urge to leap from my station, I remembered the coxswain's orders.

I need you to stay on the radio tonight.

I put my trust in my fellow crew members on deck. I knew they'd have a plan in action. The point where the female crew member had ended up wasn't the easiest place to pull a casualty onto the boat, but it was where she was heading.

They didn't have a choice.

As they drew her nearer I saw a flash of yellow, as one of the crew broke the guardrails to allow them to pull her on board. They heaved and heaved, but they didn't seem to be getting anywhere, battling the wind and waves. I could see they were struggling, and I desperately wanted to go up to help – but I couldn't leave my station.

With the situation changing from moment to moment, it was imperative that communications weren't left unmanned. I was the central point of contact for everyone.

In the end, they managed it. After a few big pulls, the woman finally rolled onto the deck. Soaked, and weak with exhaustion, she was propped up next to the wheelhouse by the crew.

My stomach was tight with nerves as I watched them regroup, ready to pull the skipper in.

As they did, I felt a wave break against the starboard side.

Oh no.

Within seconds, its impact travelled right through the boat to the port side, where the crew was gathered. The force knocked Mark Osborn almost off his feet. He'd been returning the guardrail to its position when the wave hit, but it wasn't yet back in place. I gasped as his arms flailed about and he started to wobble forwards towards the gap, almost as if in slow motion.

He's going to go in! I thought, leaping to my feet.

But just as soon as it happened, I saw the female casualty lean forward and grab him, pulling him back as she did.

She probably didn't realise it, but she'd likely saved his life. If he'd gone in at that point, it would have been extremely hard to recover him.

Thank goodness, I sighed.

Once again, though, the relief was only temporary. As I glanced back to the port side of the boat, I spotted more drama unfolding. My stomach lurched.

Dan was over the side of the lifeboat's rails, standing on the aft spray rail – a tiny ledge of no more than a toe's width. One hand clinging onto the guardrail behind him, he had the skipper of the *Paperchase* by the scruff of his neck, holding him up as best he could as the waves rolled in towards them. He was waist-deep in water and swamped by surf, so wet in fact that his lifejacket had auto-inflated.

Our lifejackets were designed to inflate as soon as they became submerged in water.

With Mark up on deck, I had no idea what the communication between the two of them had been, but it looked to me like Dan had acted on his own initiative. He'd seen his one opportunity to grab the man and he'd taken it. Because of that, though, it meant he hadn't had time to clip his harness onto the lifeboat.

He was literally holding onto the lifeboat with one hand, while holding the full weight of an adult man in his other. My heart was in my mouth as I watched from the wheelhouse.

How the hell was he doing it?

Between the sheer weight he was grasping and the force of the waves crashing against him, he was lucky he hadn't been washed right off. As the waves rolled through, his feet must have been all but slipping off that incredibly narrow ledge.

Thankfully, I saw Keith rushing towards him to assist. As he approached, Dan turned his head and started shouting.

'Clip me on! Clip me on!' he yelled.

Keith got hold of Dan's harness and clipped him onto the nearest thing he could.

The guardrail.

As soon as he was attached to the lifeboat, Dan released his grip from the rail and managed to get both of his hands to the casualty, trying to hoist him up onto the boat.

I kept one eye on Dan, as I contacted the coastguard.

'Dover Coastguard, this is Eastbourne Lifeboat. We have one person on board,' I said. 'We are attempting to recover a second.'

'Roger that. All received,' replied the coastguard.

Now totally reliant on his harness to hold him in position, I watched as Dan manoeuvred the exhausted skipper between his legs, keeping him out of the water that way. By now the rest of the crew had arrived, ready to help Dan pull the man aboard. But there was a problem.

To pull the skipper on with ease, they needed to break the guardrail – the same one that Dan was attached to.

It was his lifeline.

If they did break it, Dan would go straight in the sea.

The crew had to think quick. Dan was struggling to keep the skipper's head above water, let alone himself on the boat.

As all of this was unfolding, Mark was slowly manoeuvring the lifeboat towards calmer water at the harbour entrance.

Keith quickly clipped himself onto a handrail on the side of the wheelhouse, moved towards Dan and gripped tight hold of him. As he held on, four more crew members grabbed the skipper and pulled him through the narrow gap between the guardrails.

They'd done it!

Now they just needed to get Dan back on board.

With Keith keeping tight hold, the crew dragged Dan over the guardrails.

He was back on deck. Phew!

Finally, I was able to heave a *real* sigh of relief.

Everyone was safe and on board, but the crew of the *Paperchase* had still been through one hell of an ordeal. They were going to need medical attention.

And so was Dan.

I grabbed the VHF radio.

'Eastbourne Lifeboat to Dover Coastguard, we have three casualties on board,' I said. 'Ambulance requested to Eastbourne Lifeboat Station.'

'All received,' the coastguard replied.

As the crew attended to the two casualties, I looked backwards out of the wheelhouse. Dan was sitting on the towing bollard, lifejacket inflated and head down.

He was exhausted.

It wasn't surprising, though. What he'd just been through was akin to being put though a washing machine. If it hadn't been for his quick and selfless actions, I knew that we would only have saved one life that night.

He'd been a real hero.

With everyone on board, Mark powered the lifeboat back towards the locks at best speed. Once tied up in the lock, we were greeted by our volunteer lifeboat medical advisor, Colin McKee, a doctor in his day job.

By now, the crew had sat the two casualties in the wheel-house with me. The doctor came down to give them the once-over. We'd wrapped them in blankets and checked them over for any immediate injuries. They were both emotional and clearly worried about one another, but despite everything they had just been through, they were in good shape.

Of course they were cold and frightened. They'd also just lost their beloved yacht and all their possessions that were on it.

But they'd come home with their lives.

They were too weak to use the long ladder in the lock gate to get back to the station, so we untied and motored through into the marina and over to the fuel pontoon.

There, they were greeted by paramedics and our shore helpers, who took them to the station and waiting ambulance.

Our job was done.

As soon as my final communications were made, I climbed out of the wheelhouse and went straight to Dan, who was still sitting by the tow bollard. The rest of the crew gathered round as well.

'Well done, mate,' I said, patting him on the back. 'Are you all right?'

'I'm OK,' he said. 'Thanks.'

'We wouldn't have got him without you,' I said.

Dan simply nodded. Fresh back from the shout, it was all still a bit too much to take in.

Back at the station, it was time for us to prepare the lifeboat for her next service. We let Dan off, of course. He'd been submerged in water and holding onto the skipper for twenty minutes out there, so we sent him inside to warm up and get a hot drink.

At first, we chatted excitedly as we tidied up, washed the lifeboat down and refuelled. But as the adrenaline drained out of us, we began to slow down.

'It was like a washing machine out there,' I said as I stowed the tow rope away.

'Not half,' said Mark, yawning.

'That was a good job tonight,' said Keith.

'It was,' I said. Then I glanced at the clock and stared in disbelief. It had just gone twenty past seven.

Less than an hour since we'd launched.

'How long were we out there?' I asked.

'We were on scene for about forty-five minutes,' Mark said.

Forty-five minutes?

It had certainly felt like a lot longer.

As I headed home, the enormity of it all started to sink in. Just how much risk the crew had taken. How we'd faced huge challenges at every turn. How we'd nearly lost both Mark Osborn and Dan.

But we hadn't.

We'd all worked together brilliantly as a team, and returned safe and sound, saving two lives to boot. It was a night to truly be proud of, especially for Dan and the coxswain Mark.

In the weeks that followed, the wreckage of the *Paperchase* was recovered and brought into Sovereign Harbour. One of the RNLI inspectors came down to do some investigations into the shout. We assumed it was because we'd had to cut the tow and lost the yacht. After the investigation it transpired that the yacht had most likely been holed during her first grounding. As we'd pulled her round and she'd re-floated, she'd rolled and her keel struck the seabed, which came right through the bottom of the yacht, causing her to capsize.

There wasn't anything we could have done to prevent it.

But that wasn't what the investigation had been all about. It turns out the inspector had written his report and submitted it to the RNLI's medals committee. Not long afterwards, a letter arrived at the station.

Mark was to receive the RNLI's Silver Medal for Gallantry, for his command of the lifeboat and his seamanship that night. Dan was to be awarded the Bronze Medal for Gallantry for his heroic actions in saving the skipper. The rest of us received medal service certificates. Mine took pride of place on my wall at home, where it remains to this day.

That was eighteen years ago – and I've never experienced a shout quite like it. I've done rescues that have been rougher, longer and even scarier. But the *Paperchase* is still the one that I talk about the most.

It's not because it was a medal rescue. None of us does it for that, although the recognition is a real honour. First and foremost, we worked together brilliantly to save two lives. *That's* the main reason we do it, to save lives at sea.

But aside from that, there were so many unusual elements to the rescue. In my twenty-four years with the RNLI, it's the only time I've been on a shout where we've used a rocket line in anger and where we've had to cut a tow. As for having a crew member in the water? That's pretty rare as well. It also still amazes me just how much action was packed into less than an hour. It simply goes to prove the power of the sea and how things can change so dramatically, even close to shore and on a short job. It's a service that means a lot to me, still to this day.

In 2004, a couple of years after the *Paperchase* rescue, I moved to Poole to become a lifeboat trainer at the RNLI college, teaching volunteers how to drive the boats and how to navigate. I remained a volunteer as well, of course. I worked as a trainer, right up until 2015, until I noticed a few niggles and pains creeping into my knees. I felt it was time for a change of direction.

Picking back up on my teenage interest in the media, I applied for a secondment with the RNLI media engagement team, working at its headquarters next door to the RNLI College, to promote the work of the charity. The secondment eventually became a permanent job and I still work with the national media team today. I guess, in a way, everything came full circle.

Since I first joined 24 years ago, a lot has changed. I now have my own little family. My partner Debs and our two daughters, six-year-old Bethan and two-year-old Amber, are very much part of my lifeboat life. They're very used to me rushing off. Without their support, I couldn't still do what I do. They are my true unsung heroes, putting up with me leaving them at a moment's notice. Needless to say, my mum still worries as much about me now as she did then!

I might currently have a desk job with the charity, but I'm still volunteer crew. In fact, I'm a helm on both the RNLI lifeboats in Poole. The pager is still on my belt and, at almost forty-one years of age, it remains the best birthday present I have *ever* received. When friends see me around, they do sometimes poke a bit of fun.

'Do you wear it on your belt all the time, Dave?' they laugh.

My reply is always a resounding yes.

After twenty-four years, it's not something that's going to change – achey knees or not!

7.

REASON TO RECOVER

Roger Jackson, Exmouth 2011

Inside Exmouth Lifeboat Station it was a day like any other. Me and a few other crew members were sitting around a table near the window with a cup of tea, having our usual banter and chat. Outside, however, it was anything but ordinary.

Exmouth seafront and the Exe estuary were usually quite calm. Sheltered from the winds, they were a haven for swimmers, kite surfers and sailboats. But on 23 October 2011, it was like another world. The weather was wild, with almost gale-force winds lashing huge waves against the shore. The sight was so spectacular, we'd even noticed locals driving down to the seafront to watch the huge 'white horses' crashing up against the sea wall, spraying the white and blue seafront shelters and passing cars, and causing streetlights to sway and flicker. To say it was extreme would have been an understatement. As was often the case, the conversation in the boathouse turned to how we'd tackle the conditions, if we had to.

'It's absolutely awful out there,' Andy Williams said, looking over at me and Mark Champion. Andy was a marine engineer and Mark a commercial pilot. Both were RNLI volunteers like me.

'It would be so difficult to launch the boat through that surf,' I said.

Our trusty D class lifeboat *George Bearman I* had seen some rough conditions in her time, and I had no doubt she'd serve us well if we got a shout.

But getting her out there today …? Oof!

We'd have a job.

'Do you think we'd need extra help to steady her?' Mark said.

'You mean while the tractor reversed her down?' I asked.

Mark nodded. I brought my hand to my face as I thought deeply. Looking at the waves, without *something* holding her down we'd probably flip.

'I'd say so,' I agreed, before grabbing a biscuit from the table and picking up my tea. It was always good to have a plan, but I didn't expect to have to put it into practice today.

No one would go out in that.

Would they?

They'd have to be mad if they did.

No sooner had the thought crossed my mind than Andy stood up and started walking towards the window.

'What the hell is that?' he said. I craned my neck to look and my jaw swung open.

No way. It can't be.

'Pass me the binoculars,' I said, stretching my hand out but without shifting my gaze. I brought the binoculars up to my face and looked across the channel. Suddenly, everything came into focus and I gasped in disbelief.

It was a rigid inflatable boat, or 'RIB', as we called them. The RNLI and military had special RIBs in service, but they were also the type of boat that people bought and used for leisure. People loved them because they were exhilarating to power up and down the bay in, fun to dive from, or just ideal to take out for a day and relax in. But in this weather?

Going out in one was madness, plain and simple. Even the most experienced seaman would find keeping that thing upright a challenge.

'What the heck are they doing?' I said.

We watched, aghast, as they continued to drive further and further away from the shore, out into the swell and the gale-force winds.

I kept willing them to stop.

'Surely they won't keep going?' I said. 'Surely they'll turn back?'

It was more a hope than a question. I knew that if they continued it wasn't going to end well, and I could tell the other lads were thinking the same as me.

This was bound to cause a shout.

As the swell built, the RIB suddenly disappeared from view, obscured by the white froth of the waves. My stomach lurched as we waited for it to reappear. Moments later we heard a man's voice.

'A boat's gone over,' he said.

He was a local man and had been on the seafront watching the waves in his car when he'd seen the same RIB that we'd been watching. Like us he had his binoculars out, but from where he'd been sitting, he'd still had sight of the RIB when it disappeared from our view.

That was when he'd seen it fly up in the air and turn upside down.

'There were a few people in it. I'm sure,' he said. 'I came straight to the station.'

'Thank you,' I said.

The waves had obviously flipped the vessel like a pancake, throwing its passengers into the churning sea. Suddenly, our pagers started to ring out in unison. The coastguard had received a call from another member of the public who had also seen the boat tossed over.

Andy, Mark and I were already on our feet, in anticipation of the call we knew was inevitable. We ran to the kit room, pulled on our RNLI drysuits, our lifejackets and helmets. Within moments we were outside.

'Looks like we're going to have to put our theory to the test,' I said to Mark, as we kitted up.

The overturned RIB was relatively close to shore and it had capsized near to the entrance of the River Exe, with the sandbanks on the right-hand side making it difficult to get to. Our D class was our inshore lifeboat, and it would be our best chance of getting close enough to pick up any casualties, better than our all-weather lifeboat, which took longer to prepare and wouldn't be able to get in close among the sandbanks.

But we'd still need her back-up.

Tim Mock, the station coxswain and mechanic, suddenly appeared. He set about paging the crew again for the launch of our Mersey class all-weather lifeboat, *Margaret Jean*.

'We'll be right behind you,' he said.

I nodded in thanks, then headed out onto the beach, where shore crew were preparing the tractor to help push the lifeboat out through the surf. Adrenaline began to pump and I started running, feeling my feet pounding the sand in my boots, blood coursing through the veins in my legs and all around my body.

It was a sensation I always appreciated, because it was a miracle I still had it.

In fact, I was lucky that I still had my legs at all, after a terrible accident ten years earlier almost ended my RNLI career for good.

I'd always been an adrenaline junkie. Even living in a land-locked village near Nottingham called Burton Joyce, I'd found plenty of high-octane activities to get involved in. Water sports were my thing, inland stuff like sailing, canoeing and water skiing, but I'd always wanted to live by the coast. When the agricultural polythene manufacturer I worked for asked me to relocate to the south-west to be a sales representative for the region, I jumped at the chance.

My repertoire of water-based activities grew as soon as I moved down to Exmouth. I loved water skiing on the sea in particular. Because of my hobbies, I slipped into the coastal community with ease. I knew the water skiers, the sailors, the coastguards and, of course, some of the RNLI crew. The RNLI had always fascinated me. As a young lad I'd been very enthused by the Ladybird book *The Life-boat Men*, and the interest and intrigue never left me.

By chance, as I made my life in Exmouth, I became friends with the coxswain of the local lifeboat, Keith Graham, and his daughter, Debbie Graham. She'd broken her neck in an accident when she was in her twenties and ended up a tetraplegic, unable to move from the shoulders down, but she didn't let that get in the way of life. She was up for anything and that appealed to the adrenaline addict in me. We became great friends and I loved nothing more than to challenge her.

'Deb, if I sort it out and take you water skiing, will you go?' I asked

'Yes, all right,' she laughed. She didn't believe me; thought I was having her on.

But I wasn't.

I took her up to my old stomping ground, the National Water Sports Centre in Nottinghamshire, where the Disabled Water Ski Association was holding an event. We went on a course and before long we were skiing together. She was sitting down and harnessed in, while I held her up with one arm. With my free arm, I'd hold the handle connected to the boat and I'd be balancing on two skis. It gave her so much freedom and she loved it. She was totally reliant on me, but she trusted me implicitly.

'I trust you because you know that if I drown, my dad will kill you,' she joked. I laughed.

What a rush! Talk about a matter of life or death.

My life or death, that was.

She was right. I certainly didn't want to get on the wrong side of her dad.

I had so much respect for Deb and her family. When both she and Keith nudged me to go on the lifeboats, I listened. As much as I loved extreme sports, it was never about the risk. I got a much bigger buzz from being part of a team, a group of people going out there and putting something back into the community. The world of water sports had given me so much joy that I relished the opportunity to give back.

That was what the RNLI was all about.

Keith retired just as I joined, but I already knew the new coxswain, Tim Mock. He was in the group of guys and girls that I was friendly with.

'You're really good,' he said to me after we'd been out on the water one day. 'You could bring a lot of skills to the crew. Why don't you come and be part of us?'

Well, how could I resist?

I checked with work, who were fine about me being on-call. Then I told my family. Coming from Nottingham, they were all very 'non-boat people'. They thought I was crazy, volunteering to go out in dangerous conditions to help strangers, but they were proud too. In fact, Mum and Dad were so proud that they told everyone that I was part of the RNLI. Like with all my other hobbies, they supported me wholeheartedly

The first time my pager went off was a call to assist two sub-aqua divers who'd got caught in a tide and were drifting out to sea, unable to swim back. When it happened, I couldn't believe I was going out with the RNLI.

Blimey, Roger, I thought. *You're going out on the boat. It's real!*

I could barely contain myself. We took the inshore lifeboat, picked them up, and brought them back safe and well.

After that, I was hungry for it.

If you do eighteen months on the lifeboats, you'll do it for life, I was told, time and again.

I could well believe it. My first eighteen months passed in a flash. Being an RNLI volunteer became part of the fabric of my life and I couldn't see any reason why I would ever want to stop. But then something took place that forced my hand.

It happened on 11 September 2001, at around the precise moment that the first of the Twin Towers came down in New York, although I didn't realise that at the time. I'd just come back from Australia with work, and had some time owing, so I'd decided to indulge in my newest hobby.

Paragliding.

I'd taken a few days off and gone to Dartmoor, to go out with my paragliding school. It was my first few days of real training and I'd been loving it, until it all went horribly wrong.

It was a gorgeous morning. I was all kitted up and wearing some boots that had been provided by the RNLI. I'd just joined its new international flood rescue team, which went all over the world to help people. They'd told me to wear the boots in so I was ready if I got called out. That day had seemed like the perfect opportunity.

I got to my launch spot, walked into the wind, pulled at my canopy and felt it filling with air. It rose slowly over my head as I did my final checks, then I started to jog down the slope I'd chosen to launch from, gathered pace and then:

BINGO!

My feet were off the ground and I was gliding. Before long I was about 500 feet in the air, gliding downwards as I'd been taught. The air was flowing above and below the glider, and things were moving steadily.

My heart was racing, but in a good way.

Dartmoor looked incredible from the sky. I was lapping up the views, the solitude and the feeling of complete freedom, when – suddenly – I felt the wind get behind me.

Oh my God, I thought. *This is bad*.

It was only a split second, but I instantly knew that I was in trouble. This wasn't meant to happen. Instead of gliding smoothly, I began to plummet to the ground, down towards Sourton Tors, a collection of rocky outcrops that rose out of the moorland.

My heart was pounding. I was gaining pace and everything was spinning out of my control. Panic rose in my chest and I began to gasp, as things started to move faster and faster.

What do I do? What do I do?

I didn't even have time to review my options. I was already feet away from the jagged, menacing rocks, moments from contact.

Oh my God, I thought again, as I instinctively stuck my legs out to try to stop myself. I squeezed my eyes shut and braced for impact.

Then it all went black.

Everything after that is patchy. I don't remember the crash, I just recall opening my eyes and finding myself on the ground, on my back. There were people around and they started running towards me. It was like everything was moving in slow motion. I was dipping in and out of consciousness, eyes drooping shut, but I didn't feel any pain.

I was just red hot.

Like I was boiling in my own skin.

As my eyes fluttered open again, I tried to push people away. 'Leave me alone, leave me alone,' I said to the gathering crowd. 'I'll be fine. I'll get up in a minute.'

I was trying to get up, but people were telling me to keep still and were putting blankets over me. Looking back, I was in shock and denial. I was fighting reality and wanted to believe that I'd just had a bad fall. That I needed a moment to compose myself, before I'd get up like normal.

But I'd just plummeted 500 feet from the sky onto a load of rocks.

Everyone around me could see what I couldn't. I'd shattered my lower legs and feet, and completely de-gloved my heels.

My legs were bent all the way backwards.

I was a mess.

'You're not going anywhere, mate,' someone said gently.

I can't recall who it was, but they told me that Devon Air Ambulance was on its way. Everything seemed to happen in a series of frames. It was like I wasn't there. I felt like I was watching it all unfold in a sequence of short snippets, interspersed with darkness.

The air ambulance hovering above me. Darkness. Paramedics leaping off the helicopter and running towards me in a blur of green and yellow. Darkness. Being trussed up like a turkey and stretchered away. Darkness.

Then I was in the air. When the call had come in about my accident, Carey Wreford, a friend and fellow RNLI volunteer, had been working in the South Western Ambulance Service NHS control room, which dispatched the air ambulance. She'd heard my name and had immediately swung into action, letting my friends and family know what had happened.

I had no idea at the time, though. When I came to in the helicopter, my head almost between the two pilots' seats in the cockpit, the paramedics were opposite me.

And I was completely delirious.

'Hello, Roger,' the pilot said. 'You've had major trauma to your lower legs, so we're going to take you to Derriford Hospital in Plymouth. We'll be there in a few minutes.'

But that's miles from home.

'I don't want to go to Plymouth,' I said. 'I want to go to Exeter. It's closer for my family and friends. The lifeboat lot will want to come and see me too.'

Like I said, I was delirious.

'You're on the lifeboats, are you?' he asked.

'Yes, I am, and I want to go to Exeter.'

'Plymouth is closer and the hospital is better for your injuries,' he said. But there was no convincing me.

'No, no, no. Exeter!' I said.

Suddenly, the pilot looked down at me.

'Look, mate, it's not a bloody taxi.'

That was the last thing I remembered.

I was in the hospital for about three and a half months after the accident. I'd snapped my lower legs in two, shattered my bones, and my heels had been ripped clean off – they'd been found in the RNLI-issue boots I'd been wearing when I fell.

Well and truly worn in!

There were open wounds on both sides of both legs, and my feet were in bits. I even ended up with an infection – MRSA, the hospital superbug. After the accident, my feet and toes were pinned, plated and screwed into place. Both legs were put into steel cages that were screwed into my bones to help them knit back together. They even had to re-join my blood vessels.

It was a remarkable effort by the NHS team who looked after me. But twice in the months following my accident I was offered amputation for my right leg.

'We're making progress on your left leg,' one of my consultants said. 'But the right leg is very severely damaged. The infection means you have very little chance of keeping it.'

'But there is a chance?' I asked.

'Yes, but it's very slim. Why don't you let us take it off and we can get you back to what you were doing before?'

'No,' I said immediately.

I understood his thinking. They could do an amputation the next day and within three months I'd be up and about on a prosthetic.

I'd be able to 'get back to what I'd been doing before'.

Except I wouldn't.

Because you weren't allowed on the lifeboats with a false leg.

'If you take it off, I'll lose my lifeboat career,' I said.

While I was in hospital, it was all I thought about. I bored the nurses, doctors and consultants with my old stories and plans about what I'd do when I got back out there. It was my sole focus.

I knew it would be hard, and I knew I had a long road ahead of me. But all that pain and work was better than the other option.

Never going out with the RNLI again.

It didn't even bear thinking about. If there was a chance to save my leg, then there was a chance to save my RNLI career – and I was going to fight for it.

I got a second opinion from another consultant, Lieutenant

Colonel Nigel Rossiter. He was an army consultant who specialised in lower-leg trauma from injuries on the battle-field. I asked him if he thought he could reconstruct my mangled right leg.

'I'll give it a go,' he said. 'But I can't promise you that you will wake up with a leg.'

He was brilliant but brutally honest.

'I'm willing to take that chance,' I said.

'I'll chop out all that's dead, chuck it in a bucket, and then whatever's left over we'll work with,' he explained.

'Whatever happens, I'm fine with that,' I said. 'If it works, I'll buy you a crate of Guinness.'

We had a deal.

Not long after, I had to figure out a way to get a crate of Guinness into the hospital. Nigel managed to save my leg.

In total, I had eighteen operations, spent thirty-seven hours under general anaesthetic, and had countless skin grafts and physiotherapy at Derriford, just to get me back on my feet – and that was just the start of it all. It was a mammoth challenge, but as well as fantastic medical care and support from my family, I had my RNLI friends at my side too.

They were like an extension of my family.

Someone from the crew would come to visit me every day while I was in hospital. Carey had made sure of that, creating a special rota on the crew notice board. Even Debs took the time to come and see me, which meant the world to me. As I faced the possibility of never being able to walk properly again, she encouraged me not to give up and inspired me to keep fighting.

She knew better than anyone what I was going through.

Every single day for three and a half months, one of them would make the two-hour round trip, just to make sure I had company and wasn't getting too into my own head.

To keep me focused on getting better.

When I told them that I wanted to get back on the lifeboat one day they backed me one hundred per cent. They even gave me jobs I could do from hospital and then from the boathouse, once I was discharged. I was back at the lifeboat station as soon as it was humanly possible. I felt inspired, sitting in my wheelchair, gazing out at the sea I longed to be out on. All the guys and girls made an effort to pop in and see me when I was there too. I still felt completely and utterly part of the team.

At the time, the RNLI was just bringing in competency-based training. It was brand new, and every station needed a lifeboat training coordinator.

'You're sitting around not doing a lot,' said Tim with a cheeky smile. 'Will you be our training coordinator?'

Apparently, this was something Howard Ramm, part of the training team at RNLI HQ in Poole, had agreed to as well. He didn't want me sitting around idly. It was perfect timing.

'I'd love to,' I said.

I threw myself into it. I was so focused that we ended up winning the RNLI's UK training awards for making Exmouth the first lifeboat station in the country to become competent in the new style of training. Between my full-time job, where my employers had put me in charge of promoting the export side of the business working from home, and my role with the RNLI, I didn't have time to brood or become disheartened. The positivity and support carried me a little closer to recovery every day.

There were still hard days, though.

I'd only been out of the wheelchair for a short while and I'd gone back to my parents' house in Nottingham. I had an appointment at the local rehabilitation centre. I got out of the car and looked at the few hundred metres I needed to walk. It wasn't the distance that bothered me.

Between me and the centre entrance was a curb.

It wasn't the high part of the pavement's curb, but the lower bit, where it dips to allow people to walk on it.

As I approached it, I went to step up.

It must have only been three centimetres high, but I just couldn't lift my leg high enough to get over it.

Honestly, I could have cried.

I'll never do it, I thought. And it wasn't just about the curb. At my lowest ebb, I lost all hope.

I'll never walk properly again. I'll never run.

And then the kicker.

I'll never get back on a lifeboat.

You see, despite having two legs and being able to move them, I still wasn't guaranteed to get back on crew. I had to have a certain level of movement and ability back. I had to be fit and mobile enough to do everything I used to do. Swimming, moving equipment, pulling and carrying people.

And right now, I couldn't even step up onto a curb!

If I wasn't back to peak fitness, I'd be a risk more than a help to crew and casualty, and they wouldn't let me back on. They couldn't. Those low points felt like a punch to the stomach. They took it out of me. They made me realise how easy it would be to give up, to slide into depression and let my dreams slip away.

But just like I fought for my legs, I continued to fight for my goal.

I was going to get back on those lifeboats.

And I did. After three and a half years I bloody did it.

In 2004, I was finally deemed fit enough to re-join the RNLI Exmouth crew.

Not that I'd ever really left. Or that they'd left me.

We'd got to this point together.

There was a slowly, slowly approach to me coming back. I had to get used to the lifeboats and all our equipment again, refresh all my training and make sure that I was back up to scratch, but it didn't take much time. After waiting so long to get this far, I could put up with a few more training sessions.

Anyway, I was doing what I loved.

Things that I thought I might never do again.

I went out on the larger Trent class all-weather lifeboat at first, as she was steadier. Once I was fully trained back up, it felt amazing being a useful part of the team, being able to give something back after all the support I'd received.

My return did cause a little fuss. The local papers, radio and TV even covered the story.

Lifeboatman hails surgeons who rebuilt his shattered body after 500-foot fall, the headline read.

Photographers turned up and took photos of me on the lifeboat, proudly wearing my RNLI kit and examining the charts. I'd got into navigation while I'd been out of action, so I'd been acting as navigator and loving it. It was a wonderful opportunity for me to thank everyone who'd made my recovery possible. After the initial flurry of interest, things returned to normal, though.

My first shout back had been a straightforward job, just to tow another boat back in.

But for me it was monumental.

It was the moment I'd fought so hard for.

From crashing into those rocks, to being faced with the option of amputation, to being in hospital for three months, to being in a wheelchair, to going back to Mum and Dad's, to rehabilitation and learning how to walk again, to being able to run again, to getting the all-clear to re-join crew …

Each one had been a small goal to work towards. A mini mountain to climb. They'd all been leading to this.

Hearing that pager and being able to get up and go to help.

I'd never felt luckier, or as happy.

The feeling of appreciation and awareness of how lucky I'd been never left me. Even after seven years, I still got a buzz from the fact that I was a member of the RNLI Exmouth crew.

I embraced every shout that came in.

Whatever we were faced with I approached in the same way I'd approached my accident. Working as a team to achieve small goals, each one taking us towards our main objective.

Looking after your crew, rescuing the stricken vessel and getting everyone back safely.

That was exactly how my mind was focused as I ran and jumped into the D class that was being manoeuvred into the water by Colin May, one of our tractor drivers. Mark and Andy were already in position, sitting on either side of the front of the boat, distributing their weight to keep her steady, a technique we learned in training called 'trimming'.

They'd usually only assume those positions further out, when the sea turned choppy. But here they were still on shore and clinging on for dear life. Just as we'd discussed earlier, Mark and Andy had gathered extra help to keep the lifeboat steady. Two more members of the crew were waist-high in the water, one on each side of the boat, holding onto her so she didn't flip over.

I took the helm and focused on our first goal.

Getting the lifeboat launched.

'Right, let's go,' I said.

As we powered out towards the capsized RIB, monster waves rolled towards us. As we hit each one, we bounced high into the air. Andy and Mark shifted around each time we landed, making sure the weight was where we needed it to be, to stop us from going over.

We were a very similar type of vessel to the RIB, you see.

The RIB had gone over because it had been climbing such steep waves that it just flipped. We could easily have done the same, but Mark and Andy's skills kept us safe and upright.

Although the RIB hadn't been too far out, in the few minutes it had taken us to launch, it had been tossed around in the waves and drifted even further. But it was still in view. We were lucky that there was only one way out of the bay. A small, narrow channel that ran out into the English Channel.

Our next goal was clear.

Get to the RIB. Quickly.

We had no idea how many people were on the boat, if anyone had managed to cling on, or if they'd all floated apart in different directions. What we did know was that even the strongest swimmers would struggle in this swell.

The sea conditions and the size of the swell meant we couldn't get the D class anywhere near its top speed of twenty-five knots, but we pushed as hard as was safe. The noise of the wind and the three-metre-high waves crashing together was deafening. Every time we cut through the surf we'd be drenched, with driving rain now pushing against us as well.

'There she is,' Andy shouted, as we neared the RIB.

As I motored towards her, my heart sank into my boots. The boat was overturned and ripped to shreds. I could see it was a high-quality piece of kit worth around £36,000, maybe even more, but the sea had just torn it to pieces like it was a cheap, flimsy toy.

Where was its crew?

I could barely hear the radio, and with the waves continuing to climb to four metres high, I was struggling to keep the vessel in view. Still, I pushed forward, using full power to climb the face of each wave and punch through the crest. Time and again, we leapt off each wave and dropped suddenly into its trough. It must have only taken us five minutes, but it felt like an eternity.

When we finally arrived, what I saw made my heart leap. Four pale-faced, shivering teenagers in wetsuits, clinging desperately onto what was left of the RIB. Just one of them was wearing a lifejacket – the only one they had on the vessel.

Still, they were alive.

For now, at least.

But they were in grave danger. The sea was tossing the distraught vessel and its rapidly tiring crew around mercilessly. The waves were unrelenting. One blow too many and the men risked being separated from the boat.

And each other.

I didn't fancy our chances of rounding up four casualties sent spinning off in different directions in this sea. Looking back in the direction of the shore, I could see our all-weather lifeboat cutting through the waves towards us. It was good to know back-up was on its way.

But she wasn't here yet and she wouldn't be able to get as close into the RIB as we would. We had to get them out of the water, now. It was our third task.

Get the casualties on board …

You'd think it would be simple enough, but there was debris from the capsized boat everywhere. Fenders, ropes and buckets bobbing around. It was far too dangerous to go up alongside the wreckage.

'If we get any of that in our propellers we're done,' I said. I knew that only the engine was giving us any semblance of stability.

'Let's get as close in as we can,' I continued. 'Then we'll get them to swim over.'

'OK,' said Mark.

Now we had four smaller goals. Get as close as we could, then one by one, get the lads to swim over to us. Once Mark and Andy pulled one in, we'd go out to the end of the channel, turn around and come back, with the two of them resuming their 'trimming' duties to keep the lifeboat from turning over as we went.

As I turned among the raging waves I trained my mind on the task at hand.

Getting our first casualty safely on board.

I managed to pull the boat to within five metres of the boys, then stopped. Mark and Andy moved into position, ready to grab the first person. I got the attention of the crew and shouted instructions over to them.

'One at a time,' I yelled. 'I want you to swim out away from all the debris and the boat, over to us.'

I saw them nodding, so I continued.

'We will grab you and drag you into the boat. ONE AT A TIME.'

More nods.

'We will have to turn around, but we will come back for each of you,' I finished.

Another round of nods and we were off.

As I went along the channel, wind-driven spray was lashing my face. I turned the lifeboat, then started heading back to the RIB, watching the waves and waiting for the safest moment to punch though the crest.

When it came, we arrived at the same spot five metres from the boys.

'Now, swim!' I shouted.

I saw one lad let go of the remains of the boat and start swimming over. My heart was pounding as I watched him make slow progress towards us. His arms seemed heavy and he was clearly exhausted.

Come on, I willed.

'Just a few more feet,' Andy shouted, encouragingly.

As he struggled to make the last few strokes towards the lifeboat, I clutched the helm, keeping the vessel as steady as I could. Seeing him tire, Mark and Andy acted in a flash, reaching out to grab his outstretched arms and dragging him on board.

'We've got him,' Mark called to me.

That was my signal to go a second time.

As I returned to the RIB once more, I exhaled.

One down, three to go.

We followed the routine again and again and again, punching through the waves, shouting out instructions and pulling each boy on board as soon as they were within arm's reach.

It took us about ten minutes to get all four lads on board. They were safe but suffering from severe cold and shock.

They needed to get to hospital.

I didn't want to waste any time. Ordinarily we might transfer survivors to the big lifeboat or get the D class onto the carriage and go back onto the slipway at the station. But in these violent sea conditions, and with four people that needed urgent medical attention, it would be too time consuming. I had my final goal set.

Get these boys back to dry land and a hospital.

I turned the boat around, with Mark and Andy sitting on each side, balancing her carefully. I cranked the engine up to full power and started charging towards the shore.

I had a plan.

'I'm going to run the boat aground,' I shouted. 'Everyone hold on.'

I knew it was the quickest way to get back to shore.

'OK,' Mark responded.

All six held on tightly, knuckles turning white. I dodged and rode the waves, clasping the helm firmly, all the time watching for the right moment to let the sea take us ashore. I watched and I watched, until suddenly I saw it.

A huge set of waves bowling in.

I positioned us carefully, pointing the bow towards a spot on the beach.

We were about a mile from land and I could already see crowds gathering.

At just the right moment, I managed to get on top of one of the towering waves. It carried us into the air as we rode the crest.

For a second, everything moved in slow motion.

This is amazing, I thought, overwhelmed by a feeling of euphoria as we flew towards land, carried by the power of the sea.

What an extraordinary sight it must have been.

Well, it certainly wasn't something you saw every day!

Suddenly, I was snapped out of my moment. The waves broke, and we landed with a crash and dull thud on the wet sand. As the waves rolled away, I heard a ripple of applause growing louder and louder. It became a roar, then a cheer, then lots of cheers.

Weeeeeeeeey! Woooooo!

About a hundred people were watching from the sea wall, and we'd ended up being plonked down right in front of them.

'Blimey!' I said, looking at Mark and Andy.

'I know,' said Mark.

It was about as much as we could manage. We'd only been out for about twenty minutes, but we were physically and mentally exhausted.

We were practically silent as we returned to the station to get changed. That's when the adrenaline really kicked in. Reality hit us all at once, and we realised just how dangerous the whole thing had been.

It was delayed fear.

'My God, that was a close one,' I said, eventually.

'We could have quite easily gone over,' Andy said.

We almost had a few times, but he and Mark fought with the boat and the waves, to make sure that didn't happen.

But really, we were as lucky as those lads to be safely on shore.

It was the biggest and hairiest rescue I had ever been on.

And it still is. In October 2018, I received the RNLI twenty-year service award. I have been part of it all for twenty-two years now. I'm even Exmouth's deputy second coxswain, something I could never have dared to imagine I might achieve when I was stuck in hospital.

We get a huge variety of rescues out here in Exmouth. I've seen ships drifting towards rocks, stranded canoeists and kite surfers, missing people and people who have gone overboard. We even had a helicopter that ditched in the sea. But rescuing the crew of that little RIB still stays with me, not least because of our spectacular return to shore!

When I received my Bronze Medal for the rescue, I was told it was for my exemplary command and leadership, boathandling and tenacity. I was honoured, but I had the RNLI to thank for all of those skills and my fellow crew members to thank for the fact that I was even back on the lifeboat. Mark and Andy's Thanks of the Institution Inscribed on Vellum was more than deserved. They made it possible for us to stay upright in those dreadful sea conditions and they got those lads on board.

It turned out they were local lads who'd pinched a new boat belonging to one of their dads and taken it out. They didn't realise how much danger they'd been in until they were floating around, clinging to debris. I certainly can't criticise anyone for being a thrill-seeker, what with my high-octane hobbies, but it was a very dangerous thing for them to do. They thought they were bigger than the sea that day, but the sea showed them otherwise.

As far as I know, they've never pulled a stunt like that again.

For me, the rescue demonstrated everything about the RNLI that had made me so determined to get back on the boats after my accident. It wasn't just about the three of us in the boat that day. It was about the locals who raised the alarm, the guys back on shore, the crew on the all-weather lifeboat, my family and friends, and of course the RNLI family that supported me and encouraged me after my paragliding accident. All of them played a part in that rescue.

It probably goes without saying that I never went back to paragliding, but the RNLI remains the love of my life. It gave me the strength to overcome an accident that many told me I would never fully recover from. It gave me the courage to refuse the amputation and keep fighting, for my leg and my lifeboat career. No one pushed me more than Deb Graham to get back out on the boats. She did see me achieve my goal, but she sadly passed away in 2012 at the age of forty.

I am forever indebted to her support and encouragement. In fact, Deb and all of my RNLI family will always be a part of *every* rescue that I do, every life that I save and every person that I help as a volunteer. Because without them I wouldn't be here, saving lives at sea.

8

RACE AGAINST THE TIDE

Anthony Chambers, Portrush 2009

I was peeling a pile of potatoes in the kitchen of my home in Portrush in County Antrim, with a pot of water boiling beside me. It was just after five o'clock and my son Alistair was coming for dinner. I was expecting him to arrive at any minute. Brushing the earth from my hands and pushing the peelings to one side, I went to grab another potato.

Then, suddenly, my pager started beeping.

Whenever this happened, everything stopped. I dropped the knife, turned the heat off under the pot and grabbed my coat as I dashed out of the house.

Dinner would have to wait.

I ran down to RNLI Portrush Lifeboat Station, just a few minutes from my house. I'd been the station's full-time mechanic for eleven years, since 1998, so living close meant I was always nearby when there was a shout.

'What have we got?' I asked as I entered the station.

'There's two kids missing off the beach at Castlerock,' said

Robin Cardwell, the lifeboat operation manager. 'They haven't been seen for a few hours.'

I started pulling on my all-weather gear, ready to go out on our Severn class lifeboat. It turned out that Belfast Coastguard had already started a search. The boys' parents had become concerned when they hadn't come back from exploring some rock pools. At about a quarter to four, they'd walked west along the shoreline at Castlerock, but the boys were nowhere to be seen. With the tide coming in, cutting off their search path, they'd called 999.

The launching authority and the coastguard had decided to send out both of our lifeboats to help with the search. By half past five, the inshore D class and its crew were already powering along the five miles from the lifeboat station to Castlerock beach. We weren't far behind them. Just as we were about to set off, my phone rang. It was Alistair.

'I just got to yours, Dad,' he said. 'Where are you?'

'We're just away on a job,' I said.

'OK, see you later.'

'Aye. Shouldn't be that long.'

Alistair was more than used to me heading out on the lifeboat at all times of the day and night. I'd been with the RNLI for thirty-one years by this stage, twenty of those as a volunteer. Back then, my day job was as a service engineer, working in and around Portrush. I was usually available to go out when a lifeboat launch was requested.

Being part of the lifeboats was a family thing. It started with my grandfather, Karl, who'd been the mechanic for the first motorboat in Portrush in 1924. My dad, Gilbert, took over from him in 1947, and then my half-brother Derek, who was twenty years older than me, stepped up into the mechanic role in 1978.

I grew up around the station, helping them launch the boats down the slip while I was still in school. It was a part of everyday life for me. Then, when I was nineteen, just as Derek took over as mechanic, it was my turn to join as a volunteer. Back in those days you didn't apply to become volunteer crew – you were invited. It was an honour to all of us harbour rats!

'Anthony,' said Jo Knox, the honorary secretary, one day.

'Yes?' I replied.

'You ready to come on board with us?'

'Of course.'

It was a proud and exciting moment. Finally, I would be following in the family footsteps. I naturally went down the mechanic route, just like the three generations before me.

Portrush itself was a small seaside resort, up on the north coast of County Antrim in Northern Ireland. But the expanse of water that the town's lifeboat station covered was significant.

To the west, we worked with Lough Swilly in the south of Ireland. In the north, we'd find ourselves working with Islay lifeboat. And then there was Campbeltown to the east side of the North Channel on the Mull of Kintyre.

During the summer season we worked closely with the RNLI lifeguards, who patrolled the beaches filled with holi-daymakers, supporting them on rescues when they needed us. It was the ones that just came to Portrush for a day out that we all had to watch. They didn't realise how volatile the tides could be and would head out in a dinghy without a second thought.

It's not a paddling pool, you'd think.

But you couldn't stop them. You could only advise, watch and hope you didn't end up having to go out to rescue them.

There were pleasure craft, yachts and motorboats to keep watch over too, and we also tended to vessels from the big fishing fleet up in Greencastle, Donegal, eleven miles from the station.

Over the years we'd had incidents involving divers, canoes, airplanes and even people rock coasteering – climbing up the rocks along the coastline, then jumping off into the sea – not to mention missing people too. We were versatile, for certain. One of our most published shouts was to assist Richard Branson from his Atlantic air balloon challenge off Portrush.

And these shouts kept us busy all year round.

Missing people, especially children, weren't an unusual occurrence. It was easy to go off exploring for an afternoon and not realise the tide was creeping up on you.

But rescuing them was always a challenge. Before you could even start, you had to find out where they were.

As we headed round to Castlerock Beach, that was the question on all of our minds.

Where were these two boys?

Right now, we had no idea if they'd climbed the cliffs, gone into one of the caves along the shoreline or were even in the sea.

It was a perfectly pleasant August evening. Although the tide was coming in, the sea was calm and it was still light. But steaming around the mouth of the River Bann towards Castlerock, nearing the cliffs, there was a heavy onshore-breaking sea. In the distance we could see that a full air and sea operation was in action. Belfast Coastguard had called in teams from Coleraine and Ballycastle, local police officers and even the Irish Coast Guard helicopter.

Everyone was looking for them.

Up on the hill a crowd had gathered, and we could see the blue vans of the coastguard cliff-rescue team. Its crew was already zipping down ropes, with flashes of blue, then scaling the rock faces, searching for the boys.

With the tide coming in fast, it was a race against time.

The cliff-rescue team had started their search in the largest cave, down to the west. I knew of the caves, but I'd never really explored them. Still, it was clear that the largest cave would have been the easiest to get the boys out of.

But things were rarely that simple.

'Nothing in there,' came the feedback from the coastguard.

As the coastguard continued its search, we scoured the coastline alongside our inshore lifeboat, or 'ILB', but we spotted nothing at all. With every minute that passed without any sign, it grew more and more likely that the boys had ventured further into one of the caves.

The coxswain of the all-weather lifeboat that I was on, William McAuley, got on the radio to the helm of the ILB, Gerard Bradley.

'Let's get a closer look at that middle cave,' he said,

'It's going to be dangerous getting either of the boats in close,' Gerard said.

He was right. Although everything was quite calm, the tide was coming in and the shallow patches around the caves meant there was a risk of being carried into the cliffs or onto hidden rocks.

Together, we came up with a plan. We would launch the all-weather lifeboat's daughter vessel, the Y-boat, and use it to provide back-up to Gerard in the D class. The Y-boat was smaller and might be easier to get up close to the cave, if Gerard struggled.

'I'm going to veer down towards the cave using the anchor,' Gerard said, as he made his approach. 'Stand by.'

It was a technique called 'veering down', where the lifeboat remained head to sea, using the anchor line to stabilise the vessel and stop it from being pushed onto any hazards.

Like those rocks around the caves.

At the same time, the coastguard cliff team suspended a crew member above the mouth of the cave. Being closer in, they might be able to hear or – if we were lucky – see the boys.

Watching from the distance, we waited quietly and patiently.

It seemed to take an age for the cliff team member to be lowered down to the mouth of the cave. He dangled for a few moments, then he began to move.

Had he seen something? Heard something? I thought.

We soon had the answer. The radio crackled alive.

'They're in the middle cave and they're calling for help,' the coastguard said.

Got them!

The fact that they were shouting was a good sign. It meant they were at least compos mentis. However, they couldn't be seen from the opening of the cave, so we had no way of knowing their condition, if they had any injuries or how far back in the cave they might be.

They were probably right at the back, trying to escape the tide.

A knot tightened in my stomach. Once the tide was fully in, that cave would be completely flooded.

They'd drown.

After an initial flurry of communication and action, the radio went silent. Even though we knew exactly where the boys were, how we were going to get them out was another matter.

Despite the efforts of the cliff-rescue crew and coastguard helicopters, it soon emerged that the only way the boys could be reached was by water. But even veering down, the swell was too great for the D class to get in close, and the passage into the cave was narrow. Even if Gerard could get in close, the lifeboat wouldn't fit down there safely.

It was too narrow, even for the Y-boat.

Suddenly, I had an idea.

'Why don't we get a man in the water?' I said to William. 'Swim in to get them?'

'That's not a bad idea,' he agreed.

'How about Karl?' I suggested.

Karl O'Neill was an ILB crew member and my nephew – another relative following the family line. William put me on the radio so I could speak to him directly.

'Will you try and swim out there, see what happens?' I asked.

If he could float down into the cave with a heaving line, he might be able to pull the boys out that way.

'I'll give it a go,' he said.

I watched intently from the Severn class as Karl jumped into the water and started to swim towards the cave, wearing his drysuit and lifejacket, and clutching the rope. He was a strong young lad and a good swimmer, but even from a distance I could see that he was struggling against the swell.

First time round he didn't even make it halfway before he started to get pulled back towards the lifeboat. He wasn't giving up, though. He went back again, trying to get into the mouth of that cave.

Every time, however, he got pulled back.

My plan wasn't working.

But why?

I watched the cycle continuing for a few minutes, looking at the way the waves kept on carrying Karl back. Then suddenly, I had a thought.

His lifejacket is too buoyant!

The ILB lifejackets had flotation. If you went overboard, they were designed to make sure you stayed afloat. But in that swell, it meant Karl was just pushed and pulled by the waves.

Living on the coast, I'd been diving plenty, and I knew it was easier to move forward using the motion of the waves.

Not easy, but easier.

Under the water and the swell, rather than bobbing along the surface, you could make a bit of ground by holding onto the boulders as the water rushed past you, so you could keep your position before moving along with the next wave.

Could the same method work here? I thought.

With a lifejacket like the one Karl was wearing, he'd have no chance of getting to the cave, let alone staying there. After all, that was exactly what the lifejacket was designed to prevent.

But our lifejackets on the all-weather lifeboat were different.

They had no flotation, unless you ended up in water. Then they triggered a valve that would inflate them automatically.

But if I disabled that valve …

I looked over again, and Karl was being dragged back into the ILB, already exhausted by the swell.

I went back into the wheelhouse.

'I've got another idea,' I said to William. I took my lifejacket off and removed the automatic head, which fires the bottom off and causes it to inflate.

'If I wear this rather than the other lifejacket, I'll be more streamlined. I'll be able to swim in better,' I said. 'Get under the surface.'

'Are you sure?' he asked.

'I'm going to give it a try.'

We had to do something. It was coming up to high water. By nine o'clock the tide would be in and that cave would be flooded. Then the tide wouldn't go back out again until midnight.

We'd have a recovery rather than rescue mission on our hands.

We needed to do everything we could to get those boys to safety. William communicated my plan to Gerard while I kitted up. I pulled on my thermal undersuit, my drysuit and helmet, before putting my adapted lifejacket over my head. By the time I was dressed, Gerard was alongside us, ready for me to transfer onto the ILB.

As we motored back towards the cave, I grabbed hold of the extra lifejacket and helmet. I was going to have to bring the boys out one at a time, and they were going to need to wear these when I did.

'Pull in round there,' I said to Gerard, pointing towards an area of partially submerged rocks. Being in the shallows would minimise the amount of swimming I needed to do, so I wouldn't tire as easily.

At least, that was the plan.

I didn't have far to swim, but trying to move in swell like that would drain even the strongest swimmer in minutes. I was fit and healthy, in the gym three times a week and obviously trained to RNLI standards. But this was still going to be a huge physical challenge.

'Here OK?' Gerard asked.

'Perfect,' I said. He'd got me to within jumping distance of the shallows I'd pointed out.

I climbed from the stern of the inshore lifeboat, making sure I avoided the propeller, then started to swim towards the cave. Straight away I could feel the pull that must have dragged Karl backwards when he made his attempts to get to the cave from further out. It was strong.

Eventually, I made it to the shallows, scrambling up towards the entrance of the cave. Swimming in deep water, I finally made it inside, with the light fading around me as I did.

The sound of waves smashing into the rocks echoed around me, the water rushing into the cave with a roar and then moments later flowing back out again with force. It was easy to move forward a metre, only to be pulled back four when that water whooshed back out of the cave.

Those poor lads must be terrified.

For a moment I waited, holding onto a rock at the entrance of the cave. It was narrower than I'd imagined and it looked like it veered off to the left.

Not a straight run.

I focused on the course of the waves.

In. Out. In. Out.

Soon I knew roughly how long I had between each wave. As the next one came in, I let go of the rock and allowed it to carry me forward a metre or two. Then it started to turn, flowing back out of the cave, so I grabbed the nearest rock and held on tight.

As the waves ran backwards out of the cave, my free arm was still tucked over the spare lifejacket and helmet. I could feel the force of the water pushing against me, so I braced against it.

The I waited. Until …

Here it comes again.

As I heard the waves starting to break at the opening of the cave, I released my grip. Feeling myself propelled forward once more, I swam when I was able to, so I could inch myself that little bit further forward. Then, when the water began to retreat from the cave …

Hold on for dear life again.

It was taking time. But it was working. After five minutes, I was seven metres into the cave and at the dog-leg to the left.

This was going to be a bit more difficult.

'It's OK, I'm here,' I shouted. They probably couldn't see me, but I wanted them to know someone was coming.

With the next wave, I *should* have them in my sights.

I positioned myself ready for the next surge. My plan was to let go and swim to the left with the swell, to get as close as I could to the boys. I looked back towards the mouth of the cave again and saw the water coming in.

Here goes …

I took a deep breath as the wave rolled towards me. I closed my eyes and started to swim, pulling as hard as I could in the direction of the boys. Then suddenly …

SLAP.

I felt the cold shingle on the right-hand side of my body, the noise of the impact echoing around the cave. I opened my eyes and looked up.

I'd been pushed against the far wall of the cave.

It was much darker here, the bend in the cave blocking the fading daylight outside.

Eyes adjusting to the darkness, I looked around and spotted two frightened faces staring at me from the back of the cave, about five metres away. Both boys were thigh-high in water, and even from a distance I could see they were shivering.

They'd been in here for six hours already.

In that moment, getting them out of the cave before the tide washed in was our priority, but I was aware they could be suffering from shock and hypothermia too. I started to make my way towards them, carried the rest of the way by the next wave.

Eventually, I landed on the shingle alongside them.

'Right, lads, what are your names?' I asked.

'Reece,' said one.

'Matthew,' said the other.

'OK, I'm Anthony. I'm going to help you out of here,' I said. 'Which one of you is the youngest?'

They were both dressed the same, wearing nothing but shorts and a T-shirt. They were both just as cold and just as scared. It was the easiest way to decide who to take first.

Reece pointed to Matthew.

'Right then,' I said. 'Let's get this lifejacket on you.'

I helped him into the lifejacket and fitted his helmet on securely.

'Now you hang tight onto me, OK?' I said.

'Yes,' said Matthew, his voice trembling.

I turned to Reece.

'I won't be long. I'm only going out there. Don't worry. I will come back. I'll keep shouting too, so you can hear me.'

'OK,' he said quietly.

It was dark and noisy in the cave, and as soon as I got Matthew around the dog-leg Reece wouldn't be able to see us anymore. I didn't want to leave him, but I had to. I couldn't get them both out together.

Despite everything they'd been through, the kids were great. They both stayed calm and listened as I told them how we were going to get out and what they needed to do. I could tell Reece was frightened to be left alone, but he trusted me to come back.

And I would …

201

First, though, I had to get Matthew to the ILB. I grabbed hold of his upper body, leant backwards and started kicking. Then he started kicking too – I'd hoped it would help to propel us along faster.

But instead we just ended up kicking one another.

We weren't getting anywhere.

'Try to kick away from my legs,' I said gently.

'Like this?' he said, booting me again.

Not quite …

'A little further away, so we don't kick each other,' I coaxed. It seemed to take an eternity as we struggled through the confused seas, but finally he got it.

'That's it,' I said. 'Well done.'

After that, we moved steadily towards the mouth of the cave. Looking over my shoulder I could see the ILB and a glimpse of the coastguard cliff-rescue guy still suspended above, on standby to help if he could. The lifeboat wasn't quite as close as it was when I'd got into the water, but it was near enough.

The tide's coming in fast, so it probably isn't safe, I thought.

As we emerged from the cave, I heard a voice calling. It was Gerard.

'I'm going to throw you a line,' he said.

I turned and indicated I'd heard him with a thumbs-up, still holding tightly onto Matthew, who was gripping me tightly.

I watched as Gerard lifted the heaving line and launched it into the air. It landed just a little away from me, but I reached out and grabbed it.

'Hold on, Matthew,' I said.

I clung to the line as Gerard towed us clear of the spray and swell into safer waters. I dragged Matthew to the side of the lifeboat and the crew hauled him aboard. I stayed in the water.

'I'm going back for your pal,' I said to him. 'These guys will look after you now.'

Matthew just nodded as Gerard passed me another lifejacket and helmet.

Here we go again, I thought.

It was quarter to eight when I got back inside the cave – forty-five minutes until the tide would be fully in. Although I had the benefit of knowing where I was going this time, the wave patterns were changing and I was totally exhausted.

Still, there was no time to waste.

'I'm coming back now, Reece,' I shouted. 'You'll be all right.'

Following the same route, I used the identical technique. Watching and waiting for the waves to come in, then allowing them to carry me forward. All the time I was shouting to Reece, letting him know where I was.

Reassuring him that I was on my way back.

When I reached the dog-leg, I shouted again. 'You'll be able to see me in a minute.'

My voice rose over the noise of the water running out of the cave. Once again, I positioned myself so the next waves would carry me towards the far wall of the cave. This time, though, when they came, the pull of the water against the spare lifejacket and helmet almost drained the life out of me. As I tried to swim, my arms felt like lead.

203

When I reached the back of the cave, Reece was still locked to the same spot, eyes wide and water creeping even higher up his waist. It had only taken five minutes for me to reach him from the cave opening, but it must have felt like a lifetime, waiting alone in the pitch dark.

This time, I was struggling too. My energy was sapped and I was gasping for breath.

'You're going to have to give me two minutes,' I said. 'But I'm all right. It's all right.' At this moment I vomited with the pure adrenaline and exhaustion.

I needed him to stay calm, but I needed to grab a rest too. If I tried to swim us out in this state, we could both end up in trouble.

'OK,' he said.

Reece was brilliant. He waited patiently and quietly, while I took some long, deep breaths, in and out. Physically, I started to feel a little better. But I still needed to prepare mentally.

I focused on the goal. Getting Reece out of the cave.

'Remember what I told Matthew before?' I said after a couple of minutes. 'Kick your legs when we're in the water?'

He nodded.

'Let's go then,' I said, putting the lifejacket and helmet on him.

One more leg to go.

I steeled myself as I leant backwards and started to move my legs. To my relief, Reece started to kick with ease and managed to avoid getting his legs tangled with mine. We moved closer to the mouth of the cave with every kick, at times having to use our feet to push ourselves away from the walls of the passage out of the cave as the sea tossed us this way and that.

It was tough, but we didn't have much further to go.

'Almost there,' I said, glancing backwards.

I could see the inshore lifeboat, and this time it was in close. The swell must have died down a little so Gerard could get right up to the mouth of the cave. I heaved a huge sigh of relief. I wouldn't have to catch the line this time.

I wasn't sure I'd have the energy.

In fact, as we kicked our way towards the boat, I felt the strength draining out of me, slipping away like sand in an egg timer. I felt my grip on Reece loosening.

I'm going to have to let him go, I thought.

The lifeboat was just ahead of us and Reece was secured in his lifejacket. I knew Gerard would get him within moments. The boy would be safe.

But I can't keep on.

Despite the ordeal almost being at an end, the exhaustion was too much. I prepared to let go and let the waves take me. I knew that as soon as I did, I'd be swallowed up and drown. I just didn't have it in me to fight the waves anymore.

But just as I went to release my grip and surrender myself to the sea, Gerard launched a heaving line towards us.

It landed in the water just a few feet in front of me.

Come on, Anthony.

I mustered every last bit of energy I had to pull us towards the line.

Got it!

I gripped the rope tightly, holding onto Reece as the crew hauled us clear of the swell and towards the lifeboat. Relief washed over me as I saw Reece being lifted out of the water, then I felt arms around my torso as I was dragged into the boat too.

The next few minutes passed in a blur. As the adrenaline wore off, my body went to bits. My stomach churned as the ILB sped us back across to the all-weather lifeboat. I tried to take slow breaths to relieve the nausea, but I just couldn't fight it. Before I knew it, I was vomiting again.

Must be the exertion, I thought.

'We'll get you checked over in a minute,' Gerard said.

While I'd been getting Reece, they'd transferred Matthew to the big boat, where they'd wrapped him in blankets. When they got me and Reece on the boat, they did the same.

I was in a daze as I watched the boys being winched up into the Irish Coast Guard helicopter. After spending hours deep in water, the two of them were suffering from shock and hypothermia, so they were being taken directly to Coleraine Hospital.

Then it was my turn.

'Let's get you looked at,' said William

'I'm all right,' I said.

I was just exhausted.

I'd only been in the water for just short of an hour, but the force and pull of the waves, dragging those lifejackets and helmets and then the two boys – it had drained me completely.

The journey back to Portrush took us twenty minutes, and just after nine o'clock the lifeboats were washed down, refuelled and ready for service again. By now, the cave would have been completely flooded.

I was so relieved that we'd got them out in time.

Needless to say, I was out a little later than I'd anticipated when Alistair had called. When I got home, dinner was the last thing on my mind. I was straight off to bed, because I was due back in the station the next morning for work.

It took a few strong coffees to get going, but I made it in. While I was there, we had some visitors. Reece, Matthew and their parents. Not surprisingly, both of the boys were very quiet, but they'd wanted to pop in to the station to say thank you.

'How are you both doing today?' I asked.

'They're both recovering well,' said Matthew's mum, Pamela. 'Thank you so much for everything you did.'

'No problem,' I said, looking at the boys. 'You both did really well.'

They'd stayed calm, listened and made my job a lot smoother than it could have been.

'You're one brave man,' said Reece's mum, Gillian. 'We really can't thank you enough.'

It was a lovely gesture, and I was glad to see both lads warm, dry and well. A few days later, one of the regional inspectors came along to look at the rescue report. It wasn't unusual and he seemed satisfied with everything, so I didn't think much of it. Not even when he mentioned it might be passed to the RNLI medal committee for recognition.

Both my dad and grandfather had been on medal services, but they'd never actually received a medal. It wasn't why we did what we did. I was aware that we'd saved two lives from the cave that day. And that was enough for me. As full-time RNLI staff, that was my job – to save lives at sea.

I honestly didn't think much about the rescue after it had passed. I'd been involved in many different shouts over the years. As soon as one was done, another one came in. Big or small job, it was always the same. I'd go out, do my job, wash my boat down, put it back in the water and then move on.

That's just what I did.

The call came about three months later, in November 2009. I was in the boathouse on my own when the telephone rang. It was a chap from RNLI headquarters in Poole.

'Is that Anthony Chambers?' he asked.

'Yes,' I said.

'I'm calling to let you know that the medal committee meeting has just finished,' he began.

The what committee …? I frowned.

It was only after a second or two that I remembered what the inspector had said about passing the report to the committee.

'Oh, right …' I said.

'We're awarding you the RNLI Bronze Medal for Gallantry,' he said. 'Congratulations.'

'Oh, well, thank you,' I said.

I was so shocked that I didn't really know what to say. The feeling was difficult to explain. I'd never wanted to win a medal. A medal rescue usually meant that someone had ended up in real difficulty, that RNLI crew had put their lives at risk. It wasn't something I aspired to. In the end, I felt proud but also very strange to be recognised for just doing my job.

That was eleven years ago. On 29 February 2020, after forty-two years' service, I retired from the RNLI. My wife Maryna and I still live in Portrush with my son, Alistair, and my step-daughters, Jessica and Louise.

Funnily enough, six years ago, before we even met, Maryna volunteered as an RNLI fundraiser. In 2014, she accepted a cheque from Limavady Boys Brigade because two boys had been rescued from a cave in Castlerock. Who presented the donation to her?

Matthew and Reece.

Such a small world, and a wonderful coincidence.

The Chambers lifeboat legacy now continues through my nephews Karl, who was out with us the day we rescued Reece and Matthew, and Jason Chambers, who was my assistant mechanic. Karl even spoke to the local paper about our family history with the service.

'Ever since there has been an engine in a Portrush lifeboat there has been a Chambers on it,' he said. 'It's all our family knows, and wearing a lifeboat pager for me is as natural as wearing a watch. It doesn't matter what the weather is doing or what time it is, when that pager goes off, we go.'

He had it spot on.

It's been a wonderful career, but living your life tied to the pager can be challenging, so I've decided it's time for me to do a bit more travelling and take my two Border collies, Poppy and Troy, with my wife Maryna on some nice long walks further afield than Portrush.

It's great to see the enthusiasm and commitment from me and my half-brother, my dad and my grandfather, passed down to Karl and Jason. They're excellent lifeboat crew and perfectly capable of carrying on the Chambers lineage. Long may it continue!

9

STORM ON THE SANDBANKS

Aileen Jones, Porthcawl 2004

I moved swiftly around the classroom, helping the children to tidy away the jigsaws, LEGO bricks and crayons they'd been using at playtime.

'OK, Tiddlers,' I announced. 'Once everything is away, sit in your places, ready for story time.'

'Tiddlers' was what we called the children in our local school's nursery class, just like little baby fish.

Fitting for a seaside town like Porthcawl.

'Yes, Mrs Jones!' they chorused happily in unison.

As they toddled to their seats and the room began to fall silent, I pulled a copy of *We're Going on a Bear Hunt* from the shelf, turned the page and opened my mouth to start reading. At exactly that moment, a familiar sound pierced the air in the classroom.

BEEP BEEP, BEEP BEEP.

I looked down to my waist and saw the flashing screen of my RNLI pager.

Crew assemble, the message read.

I looked back up to see twenty faces staring at me excitedly.

'Are you going out on the lifeboat, Mrs Jones?' one child asked, eyes wide with curiosity.

'I'll have to go to the station to find out,' I said, leaping to my feet.

They might only be three and four years old, but when my pager went off, they knew the drill. In fact, the whole school did.

You see, it was a regular occurrence in our seaside community in Bridgend in Wales. Generations of kids from our town grew up watching people of all professions dropping everything to go out on the lifeboat.

Everyone knew what to do when the pagers went off.

At the nursery, my boss, Mrs King, would appear, as if by magic, to take over the class.

'You be good for Mrs King,' I'd always say, before grabbing my coat, dashing to my car and driving off in the direction of RNLI Porthcawl Lifeboat Station. Across town, my fellow crew members would be doing the same.

Of course, call outs didn't just come during working hours. They could happen at any time, from first thing in the morning, before you'd even had a coffee, to the middle of the night, when you were sound asleep.

I loved that buzz, the feeling you could be called on at any moment. I loved the unknown. You never really knew what to expect on a shout, you see. You just had to get there, look at the situation and work together with your crew to deal with it.

We saw plenty of broken-down speed boats and fishing boats in Porthcawl. During the summer months, we were forever rescuing windsurfers and kite surfers stranded on rocks after they'd been carried down the coast on what we called the 'Rest Bay Bus', a vicious riptide that would pull them along from the Rest Bay two miles away, right along into Porthcawl.

But the real danger lay in our sandbanks.

To the naked eye, our little harbour was picturesque and calm. But beneath the surface it was full of hidden dangers. Large ships steered clear of us but smaller boats would sometimes chance passing through to cut journey times.

Always a big mistake.

When the tide was low, parts of the bank would dry out and create little beaches right in the middle of the channel. On calm days it would be fine, and vessels could avoid hitting the banks, just like they avoided the shoreline.

But on rough days, it was a different beast. If a boat got caught in the surf crashing on the sand, they'd get rolled down the bank as if they were in a washing machine.

Over the years the sandbanks had proved deadly.

That's why, when the pagers went off, time was always of the essence.

If the call came when I happened to be working, I'd be at the station in a flash. I'd pull on my drysuit, orange lifejacket and Gecko helmet, and be ready to tackle whatever was waiting for us within minutes. My lifeboat station dashes were so frequent that a fellow crew member, Chris Page, set up a webcam that connected directly to the lifeboat station. My big sister Alison, a local coastguard who also worked at the school, would play the footage whenever there was a shout, so the children could see exactly what happened and understood the important work the RNLI did in their hometown.

I always made sure to glance up and give a quick wave.

They got ever so excited.

Because, in the blink of an eye, I'd transformed from Mrs Jones, the nursery nurse, to Aileen Jones, RNLI helm.

I'd been the station's second female crew member when I joined in 1995. Now I was the station's first ever female helm too.

In fact, I was one of the first in the whole of the RNLI.

There'd been some fuss and fanfare when it happened, and I was more than a bit chuffed. But being a 'first' wasn't something I thought about much. I'd never set out to be pioneering.

That said, I guess the fact that I was a woman meant my route onto crew had been a little different to my male counterparts. While most of the lads came through Sea Cadets and joined the crew as soon as they were seventeen, I'd only joined at the age of thirty.

It wasn't for want of trying, though.

I think I was always destined to be out at sea. I was a proper tomboy growing up, always out in Porthcawl harbour on my dad's little sailing boat, riding my bike by the lifeboat station or just hanging around the seafront in jeans and trainers, marvelling at the ever-changing twists and turns of the tide.

The minute I was allowed, I joined the Girls' Nautical Training Corps, the girls' section of the Sea Cadets, and I wanted nothing more than to join the team at RNLI Porthcawl, just like my brother-in-law, Phil.

He was nine years older than me and already on crew. He and my big sister had moved back into the family home just after they got married, while they waited to move into their new house.

Living with Phil was a golden opportunity for me.

And a pain in the backside for him.

If the maroons went off in the morning or the middle of the night, I'd grab my clothes, leap out of bed and sprint to the bathroom. More often than not, I'd beat him to it.

'Not again, Aileen!' he'd shout, as I slammed the door behind me.

When I came out of the bathroom, fully dressed, I'd be grinning cheekily. He, on the other hand, would be less impressed.

'Out of my way now,' he'd huff, ushering me to one side.

While he was doing his business, I'd be doing mine.

Getting myself buckled into the passenger seat of his car.

By the time he emerged from the house, I'd be there waiting.

'I'm coming with you,' I'd say.

He never had time to argue. He'd roll his eyes and off we'd go.

It became a game of cat and mouse. But even if he outwitted me, I'd just hop on my bicycle and follow him down anyway.

I must have been a real nuisance.

I got told off all the time, but I always took it as an opportunity to learn. One day, Mr Roberts, the deputy launching authority, gave me a right row when he saw me carrying a lifejacket inside after the crew had been out on a shout.

'Aileen, you'll damage that if you're not careful,' he said.

I looked down and noticed the buckles dragging on the floor.

'Sorry,' I said, cheeks reddening as I scooped them up.

I never did it again.

Any excuse I could find, I'd be there, watching, listening and asking questions. And just after my seventeenth birthday, I had a very important question for the crew's honorary secretary, a job we now know as lifeboat operations manager.

'Please can I join the crew?'

I could sail, I was fearless and I was more than happy to do all the training I needed to make the grade. Why wouldn't they let me?

I couldn't see any reason why not.

I completed all the application forms, sent a formal letter and waited. A few weeks later, after pestering the crew on a daily basis, I got my reply.

We're not looking for new crew at the moment.

I was gutted. But I accepted the honorary secretary's decision.

I never for a moment thought that it was anything to do with my gender. After all, I knew through the Girls' Nautical Training Corps that there were a few female crew members at Atlantic College Lifeboat Station over in the Vale of Glamorgan.

Not many, but they existed.

Despite the rejection, the lifeboat station still felt like home to me, so I stuck around.

As it does, life really picked up pace after I left school. In what felt like the blink of an eye, I was soon married with two beautiful children. Our girl, Frances, arrived first, followed by our son, Daniel, four years later.

My husband Stephen and I had been set up on a blind date. When we first met, he'd had nothing to do with the RNLI, but that didn't last long. Between us, Phil and I convinced him to join as a helper – what we call 'shore crew' nowadays.

'I'm not sure if it's for me,' he'd said.

'You'll enjoy it,' I insisted.

I had ulterior motives, of course. With two young children and my job at the nursery, I couldn't even imagine having the time or energy to be on crew. But wives and girlfriends of crew were invited to everything.

I could still be part of it that way.

And I was. I helped at fundraisers and socials, and carried my own VHF marine radio around with me everywhere, so I could hear all the communications from ship to shore and back again. This became even more handy when Stephen was inevitably bitten by the bug and moved from shore to boat crew. I always knew what he was up to. At times I felt like my little family spent more time at the station than at home, and I was happy with that.

I didn't even think about my childhood dreams to get on the crew. Until one day, a woman finally joined RNLI Porthcawl's shore crew.

Her name was Wendy, and she worked alongside the lads, preparing kit and driving the tractor to help launch the boat.

I'd never been so excited.

Daniel was just about to go off to nursery, and I had time to think about things outside of family life for the first time in years. Watching Wendy claiming her place on the crew inspired me. Almost thirteen years after my application had been declined, I couldn't help but wonder.

Was now my time?

Turns out it was.

Although Wendy only stayed for a year, she shoved her foot in the door and left it open a crack for me.

With Frances busy at school and Daniel happy staying with his grandparents when he wasn't in nursery, I joined the shore crew and spent all of my spare time at the station.

I was there so often that one day my friend Steve Williams turned to me.

'Why don't you just go for crew, Aileen?' he said.

I don't know why, but my stomach flipped at the thought.

'Do you think I'll get on?' I asked.

Steve had known me since I was a kid and had been at the receiving end of my bothering for decades.

'You've been around long enough,' he smiled. 'It's probably about time.'

When I finally went for it, the crew couldn't have been more supportive, encouraging me every step of the way.

Probably looking forward to me making myself useful, I thought.

In many ways, starting later worked to my advantage. I progressed through the various levels of training uninterrupted by maternity leave or having very small children at home. I was able to really throw myself into it.

When I finally made Porthcawl lifeboat crew, it rarely

occurred to me that I was one of a very small number of female volunteers, let alone lifeboat crew members.

I hardly noticed that I was the only girl on crew in Porthcawl, either.

Instead, it was silly things that brought the lack of female crew to my attention. Like the time I found myself in a ladies' changing room on my own after some off-site training in Cowes on the Isle of Wight. There were people from crews all over the country, but not a single other woman.

They didn't know what to do with me.

Being isolated from the banter and the camaraderie was so strange. I had half a mind just to barge into the gents and change there. But I had no idea how they'd react.

Back in Porthcawl, I'd pile into the same changing room as the lads. I wasn't shy and none of my guys batted an eyelid. Even if I had a skirt on, which was *very* rare, I'd simply nip behind a curtain to shuffle my drysuit on.

The only problem I had in my home station was that the kit didn't fit me well. Our drysuits weren't built for women's bodies and the smallest boots were a size eleven, dwarfing my size-three-and-a-half feet.

Everything was huge on me.

But it was a small inconvenience. I was just happy to be doing what I loved. Things changed over time, of course, and eventually we got suits made especially for women.

No more schlepping along in giant boots for me!

More and more women joined. I saw my 'Tiddlers' from the nursery turn up in shore and boat crew. Strapping lads *and* strong girls forming fantastic young crews. Even my daughter Frances joined.

Yes, I worried about her. But I worried about me and Stephen too. In fact, we agreed to never go out on a shout together.

Just in case anything happened.

It was a dangerous vocation, no doubt about it. But we were all highly trained, we had excellent equipment and we were a community that looked out for one another, at sea and on land.

In my opinion, there were far worse places for kids to be.

By the time I'd been helm for six years, most of the family worked or volunteered out at sea. There was me, Stephen, Frances, her cousins and loads of our friends. Phil was still there too, and even though he and my sister had separated, we all still got on.

Daniel still had four years before he could join, but he was already a little mini-me, hanging around the station.

It was only a matter of time.

I was immersed in the lifeboats and I was always 'on'. Especially when the weather turned, just like it did on 24 August 2004. The howling wind and rain instantly transformed Porthcawl's dormant sandbanks into a shape-shifting obstacle for fishermen, jet skiers, windsurfers and whoever else had the misfortune to find themselves caught up in the waves.

I understood all too well why some locals called them 'widowmakers'. Over the years, many lives had been lost on those banks, so as the sea began to roll, I was on high alert.

My mum and sister had travelled from Wales to Ilfracombe in England, for a few days away. Dad had decided to join them later. I'd offered to give him a lift to the ferry terminal, so he could jump on *The Balmoral*, a boat that made the journey over to Ilfracombe a few times over the summer months. But it wasn't the day we'd been expecting. The forecast had been for blazing sunshine and high temperatures across the UK. But it seemed that Porthcawl didn't get the memo.

As we neared the terminal, I looked out at the waves, frothing angrily into what seemed like an infinite number of watery peaks, and I shuddered. I wasn't keen on the idea of Dad getting on the ferry.

It was conditions like this that conspired to get boats like The Balmoral *in trouble.*

When we arrived, I stepped out of the car, pulled my coat around me and raised my collar to act as a windbreaker. It was freezing, and the wind made walking even a few feet quite the challenge.

No sign of that mini heatwave we'd been promised.

As we neared the terminal building, I spotted a sign saying that the ferry had been cancelled. It was finishing its last service, then docking until the weather improved. I can't tell you how relieved I was.

'It wouldn't be safe out there today,' I said to Dad, as we turned on our heels and fought our way back to the car.

'It is pretty bad,' Dad agreed.

Rather than go straight home, though, Dad and I sat in the car and watched *The Balmoral* in the distance. The wind shook the car as it rumbled around us. The boat's skipper would no doubt know these waters like the back of his hand, but *The Balmoral* appeared to be going all the way along the bank, rather than cutting across as normal.

It really must be bad out there, I thought.

From where we were, I couldn't see much else out on the water. Fishermen and sailors who knew the area well would probably have avoided going out in these conditions, knowing how volatile it was around those banks. And novices and holidaymakers?

Well, it wasn't really the weather for a day trip.

But watching white foam erupting over the sandbanks, I turned my trusty VHF radio up loud.

Just in case. You just never could tell when someone would find themselves in trouble.

Eventually, we set off home. I'd barely been in the house five minutes when a familiar voice crackled from my radio. It was Gordon Woosnam, the skipper of a local boat called the *Gower Pride.* I stopped and listened carefully.

He was communicating with the coastguard.

'I'm in real trouble here,' he said, his voice panicky.

My stomach flipped. Gordon was a pretty proficient seaman and he knew the area well.

If he was struggling, it must be bad out there.

He hadn't yet called for assistance, but I'd been RNLI crew for long enough to know what came next. I pulled my coat back on and headed to the door.

'I'm going to the station,' I shouted to Dad as I left.

When I arrived, I was the first helm at the station. If we did get a call out, it would be me commanding the crew of our Atlantic 75 class lifeboat, *Giles.* I stared anxiously out to sea, eyes trained on the distant outline of the *Gower Pride,* a nine-metre fishing vessel, watching it bounce and roll among the waves. I was anxiously waiting for the inevitable.

Then the call came. It was the coastguard.

'We have the *Gower Pride* in difficulty,' he said. 'There's an injured crew member as well. Can you launch?'

'We're on our way,' I said.

As the launch authority sent out the signal. My pager beeped, just like others across town.

BEEP BEEP, BEEP BEEP.

Within minutes, volunteers were streaming into the station. Looking outside I could see the waves breaking over the pier. The wind was howling and by now I was struggling to spot the *Gower Pride* among the surf and swell.

I needed to pick my crew. Ordinarily, I would take two members out with me.

But these were no ordinary conditions.

Controlling the lifeboat would be tricky in this sea. I'd need all the eyes I could get on potential hazards, not to mention an eye on the location of the fishing vessel.

The tide was ripping along, pulling him further and further away.

'We're going to need all the help we can get today,' I said to Simon Emms, as I picked him to join my crew. I stood the remaining volunteers down.

Even though they weren't coming out, I knew the other volunteers would do everything they could to support us from shore.

Just ten minutes after the call, we launched.

As we hit the water with a splash, after having been pushed down the slipway by the station's tractor, I could feel the swell immediately. Three of us were positioned inside the boat. I could see Mark Burtonwood, a local student, gripping his seat, and Simon sat on the side of the lifeboat, clinging on as we picked up speed out into the harbour.

It was rough. Really rough …

The waves started to pick up almost immediately. Rather than gliding along, the lifeboat was bouncing around and riding the surf. As I steered, I suddenly realised that I'd lost sight of the *Gower Pride*. My heart sank, praying that she had not been rolled over by the twenty-foot swells I could see in the distance.

'I can't see where she is,' I shouted.

The crew took control of the radio.

A brief moment of relief washed over me when I heard Gordon's voice. But he didn't sound good. Although he was trying to clarify his position, he was in such a state of panic that our crew had to cut in.

'Slow down, skipper,' they said.

'I've broken down and I'm drifting,' he said, speaking as clearly as he could. 'My crewman has a broken arm.'

We reassured him that we were on our way.

My heart started to race and I felt the adrenaline really kick in. The boat had no engine. That meant it could be moving helplessly towards any one of the deadly sandbanks, unable to power away and fight the currents.

Determined, I narrowed my eyes and focused on the task at hand. We trained and trained and trained for days like this.

Sailing in challenging seas, learning how to tow stranded vessels and everything in between.

Now it was time to knit it all together.

Calling my crew together, I laid out a plan. When we reached the boat, our first priority would be to get her away from the sandbanks. We could only do that by towing her away ourselves.

'We'll need to get a line to the skipper and establish a tow when we locate the vessel,' I said. 'After that we'll assess the situation again.'

The guys nodded in agreement. Everything could change in a heartbeat out at sea, so we took our goals one by one.

Now to find the boat.

As we motored along the north side of the East Nash sandbanks, I could see waves double the height of the vessel rising and falling. It was no wonder we were struggling to find her. A sea this rough could swallow up a boat of that size.

One with no engine, that is.

Calmly and methodically I scanned the area that correlated with the location Gordon had given us, expanding my search to take into account the direction of the waves that would be pulling him along. Then, finally, I spotted her.

She was being tossed around like a rag doll in the distance, on the opposite side of the bank.

But we had eyes on her.

'On the south side,' I said.

Bringing the crew together again, we looked at our options.

'We can't cut over the bank in this weather,' I said.

We'd find ourselves having the same problems as *Gower Pride* if we did that.

'We could go the long way,' suggested Mark. 'Around the Nash passage?'

'Great idea,' I said. 'I'll go towards the lighthouse, then we can go around the bank.'

'Let's go,' said Simon.

Adrenaline was still coursing through my body as we came through the Nash passage. The waves were building, climbing higher by the minute, as the wind plucked at them. I held on tight to the helm as I concentrated on getting to the boat. As we rode along though the surf, I could see the lads clinging on tight as well. The lifeboat was on end, balanced almost upright on our engine as we see-sawed over the waves.

In all my years, it felt like the hardest I'd ever pushed our Atlantic 75. I was in control, but I knew she was at her limits.

We can't do this alone, I thought.

'We're going to need assistance,' I shouted to the guys.

'Definitely,' Mark agreed.

We radioed our operations manager.

'Requesting assistance from the Mumbles lifeboat,' he said.

The Mumbles crew had *Ethel Anne Measures*, the Tyne class all-weather lifeboat, a real powerhouse of a vessel. If we could secure the boat, they'd be able to tow her back faster and more safely than we could.

Moments later it was confirmed.

'The Mumbles lifeboat is launching,' the coastguard said.

It was good to know we had back-up on its way, but we knew it would take them at least an hour to reach us. We weren't going to wait around.

We couldn't.

If we left the *Gower Pride* drifting without a tow, it could end in disaster. We had to continue with our original plan.

As we powered on into the driving wind and rain, the *Gower Pride* finally came clearly into view.

Gordon, the skipper, wasn't on the back of the boat, but he saw us.

'Am I glad to see you,' came Gordon's voice over the airwaves.

And me you, I thought.

Straight on with the plan, the crew radioed him back.

'We're going to throw you a line.'

It was going to be a risky manoeuvre. To get the line over and give Gordon the best chance of catching it, I needed to get as close to the *Gower Pride* as possible – but not so close that the boats would collide.

On a normal day, that wouldn't be a problem. But today's unpredictable sea conditions meant a sudden swell could throw us together.

I took a deep breath and clutched the helm, as Gordon emerged up onto the sodden deck of the *Gower Pride*. He looked exhausted and his face was ashen. As he tried to scramble to the bow, the waves bounced the boat up and down like a bath toy, water engulfing the deck each time.

This must be horrendous for him.

'It's coming over,' Simon shouted, as he tossed the line over the side. I held my breath as I watched it fly through the air, as if in slow motion.

Catch it, Gordon, I thought.

He did. As soon as it was in his hands, he was on his knees, tying the line to the bow.

'Well done,' Mark shouted over, as we prepared to pull away.

I felt the reassuring backwards pull of the *Gower Pride* at our stern as we slowly began to tow the boat back to the station. We weren't out of the woods yet, but with the tow in place at least we could get him away from the …

Suddenly, something stopped my thoughts in their tracks.

I felt pressure falling away from the lifeboat. The backwards pull was gone.

I knew immediately what had happened.

'We've lost her,' I shouted.

The line had parted and was now dangling in the water.

The rope can't have been tied tightly enough.

Now the fishing boat was drifting away from us again, back towards the sandbanks.

OK, time to reassess the situation.

I called my crew together.

'We need to get one of you on there,' I said.

It wasn't something we'd usually do. Certainly not in these conditions. It meant putting the boats even closer together, and that was dangerous. But lives were at risk.

If we relied on the skipper to tie the tow, the same might happen again.

We'd only get so many chances.

The skipper was fatigued and struggling after battling with the elements for so long already. He might not have the strength left to get up to the bow and tie the line again. With one of us on there, I knew it would be properly secured, and the skipper and his crewman would be in safe hands.

'I'll give it a go,' Simon volunteered.

'Great, let's do it,' I said.

In agreement once again, we assumed our positions.

It took everything I'd learned about controlling our vessel to turn the lifeboat in those rising waters and get safely up alongside the fishing boat. By the time we caught back up with him, he was more or less where we'd started from initially.

Too close to the bank for my liking.

As we approached, waves crashed against us and I watched in horror as a buoy hit Mark on the head.

I gasped audibly, as I momentarily prepared to have another casualty to consider.

And one less pair of hands and eyes.

Thankfully, his helmet had protected him.

'I'm fine,' he shouted, immediately

Thank God for that.

Crew regrouped, Simon scrambled to the port side of the lifeboat, clutching a tow line and radio. Then, as we came up alongside the *Gower Pride*, he sprang up like a jack-in-a-box, grabbing hold of the vessel and clambering aboard. Holding my position, I gave Simon time to steady himself. Then Mark threw over a first-aid kit.

Once we got the line sorted, he'd be able to attend to the injured man.

He set to work immediately. With the boat still bobbing violently, he crawled up the deck and firmly tied the line to the bow, before giving a thumbs-up.

Second time lucky, I thought, as we began to tow.

I felt pressure, and the *Gower Pride* began to move behind us.

This time the line held firm.

But we had a new challenge to tackle.

At the speed we were travelling, battling against the elements, the tide would have gone out by the time we got back.

How were we going to do this?

As if on cue, the Mumbles lifeboat arrived at the scene. I don't think I'd ever been more relieved to see our colleagues from down the coast. The *Gower Pride* was rolling dangerously and even the Mumbles all-weather boat itself was taking a battering, rails dipping underwater as she approached.

'We're going to throw our line over to the boat,' coxswain Martin Double said over the radio. Simon heard the plan too. Moments later he appeared on the deck of the *Gower Pride*. There wasn't much for him to hold onto. What was there was slippery as an eel, so he had to crawl bravely along the boat to the bow to grab the line.

It was quite a sight to behold. My heart was in my mouth, worried that he'd be swept off deck, but Simon took it all in his stride.

It was probably only a matter of minutes, but it seemed to take an eternity to make the connection this time. The Mumbles crew tossed the line over again and again. Until, finally, Simon had it.

Without missing a beat, he tied the new line and released ours, before making his way back down below to attend to the crew. By one o'clock, two hours after the initial call, we were bringing the *Gower Pride* in.

But we weren't home and dry yet.

Even with the more powerful all-weather lifeboat on the case, there was a chance that the line could part and we'd have to start the whole song and dance again. We were also racing against the tide. If the Mumbles crew had been able to use both engines, they'd have been home in a jiffy, but they couldn't.

The movement would have tossed the *Gower Pride* right over.

Instead, they had to use just one engine.

It was cutting it fine, but it should be just the right amount of speed …

Or so we hoped.

It was a nail-biting journey back to the shelter of Porthcawl Pier. We followed behind on standby the whole way, just in case the fishing vessel became detached and started drifting again. It was only when *Ethel Anne Measures* moored up on the pier and the injured crewman was whisked away in a waiting ambulance that we could really heave a sigh of relief.

They were safe.

Back at Porthcawl Lifeboat Station, spirits were running high.

'That was one hell of a shout,' Simon whooped.

'I know. Well done all of you,' I said. Adrenaline was still pumping through my body and my hands were shaking.

'We did really well,' said Mark. 'Especially Spiderman over there.'

We all looked at Simon and laughed. He'd certainly shown off some 'spidey skills', crawling over that deck and tying those lines.

Not to mention skill and bravery.

But I never expected any less from my crew.

They were all amazing.

That said, it did still feel like an extra-special rescue. On the surface, it was quite routine. A broken-down boat needed towing in. But in those conditions, it was something else, far more dramatic than others I'd experienced. We'd had to call on all of our training and past experience, test our skills to the limit and work together to make the right decisions as quickly as possible.

The success wasn't just down to us either. It was the operation managers and coastguard, our shore crew and the Mumbles RNLI guys. We'd all come together to make something really special happen.

Every single one of them was a hero to me. None of us could have done that rescue alone.

We were a team.

We'd gone out, each done our part and got everyone back safe.

It was the greatest feeling.

Even after the most dramatic of rescues, everything soon returns to normal. Weeks and months passed in a blur of work, regular training at the station and family life. Then one week in November, about three months after the *Gower Pride* rescue, something odd started happening.

RNLI head office was constantly calling the station to speak to Phil. Out of the blue, we started getting phone calls from journalists asking about the *Gower Pride*.

'That was months ago,' I frowned, after hearing of another call.

I was more than happy to shout about what we'd all achieved that night. But why now?

A few days later, I was doing a forest school course with work when I got a call. It was Phil.

'Can you come to the station this Thursday, Aileen?' he asked.

'Sure, what's happening?' I asked.

'We're just having a bit of a get-together,' he said. 'Bring Stephen and the kids too.'

I'll admit, I was suspicious. If there was a social, I'd usually know about it well in advance.

I knew they were up to something, but I couldn't put my

finger on it. Not that it mattered anyway. I was always keen on a social event at the station. On the night, I was having a fantastic time chatting and mingling, when Phil stood up to make an announcement.

'We've brought everyone together to share some wonderful news,' he said. 'The RNLI medals committee has decided to recognise some members of our crew for the *Gower Pride* rescue earlier this year.'

Everyone knew that the medals committee met quarterly to select crews and individuals to be recognised, but you never imagined getting picked.

Wow. This is big, I thought.

I couldn't help but beam with pride as we heard that Simon was to be accorded the Thanks of the Institution Inscribed on Vellum for his courage and determination. Mark was also to be presented with medal service badges and certificates. These accolades were some of the highest honours you could receive from the RNLI.

And by gosh did they deserve them.

I was so wrapped up in the moment that what happened next almost knocked me off my feet.

'Finally, Aileen Jones will be presented with the RNLI's Bronze Medal for Gallantry.'

My jaw hit the floor, as the room erupted into cheers.

A gallantry medal?

I was gobsmacked. The committee had chosen me to be recognised for my 'courage, seamanship and leadership'. I'd never felt more honoured in my life.

I was still in a shocked daze when our retired operations manager, John Williams, came up to me.

'I don't think I've ever heard of a woman getting a medal, you know,' he said.

'Don't be daft. I bet there have been loads,' I said.

I'd read enough about the RNLI's history to know about 1830s heroine Grace Darling, who'd rowed out from Bamburgh, on the coast of Northumberland, to rescue survivors from the wrecked steamship *Forfarshire*.

There were bound to be more as well.

'But was she crew?' he asked, when I suggested the example.

I had no idea. But a few days later, RNLI head office got in touch with the answer. I wasn't just Porthcawl's first female helm anymore. I was the first *ever* female RNLI crew member to receive a medal.

I was presented with my Bronze Medal by the Duke of Kent in the Barbican Centre in 2005. After that, even more amazing experiences opened up to me. I retired from crew at the age of forty-eight, but in 2010 I became one of the RNLI's first female launching authorities. Then in 2016, I was recognised in the Queen's birthday honours.

I have to admit, when I saw that I'd been sent a letter from the Cabinet Office, my first thought was, 'Oh no, what have I done?' So finding out that I was being awarded an MBE was an incredible surprise and relief!

If you told that boat-obsessed teenager hanging around Porthcawl Lifeboat Station that one day she'd go to Buckingham Palace to receive an MBE, she'd have laughed in your face – especially if you told her that she'd be wearing a skirt and high heels for the occasion.

Navigating a proper curtsey in front of Prince William, the

Duke of Cambridge, was scarier and more difficult than any seas I'd navigated.

But I loved every minute.

When I stepped up for the presentation, Prince William spoke.

'You're not wearing your ...' He paused and indicated an imaginary pair of braces.

'Salopettes?' I ventured.

'Yes, salopettes,' he smiled.

'I'd much rather have worn those,' I replied.

'I've flown over your area many times, you know,' he said. 'Congratulations on all your work.'

'Thank you,' I said. Then I turned around and beamed at Stephen, Frances and Daniel as I made my way back to my seat. It was a magical moment. One I will never forget.

Volunteering for the RNLI has been a lifelong pleasure for me. A hobby, a way to spend time with my family and a way to give back to my community. I never set out to be pioneering. I was never trying to pave the way for women in the RNLI. I was just doing what I love, but it's been a wonderful side effect of a very happy twenty-five years volunteering.

The pioneering bit was a happy accident.

I'd still love to be on the boat now – and I'm capable too – but you have to make way for the young ones. My role as launching authority is a whole new test of my skills. It's my call if the crew go out or not. It's a responsibility that challenges me in brand new ways. It's a crucial decision every time, and I think my years of experience serve me and the crew well.

It took a long time before I realised the true impact that I and other early female RNLI crew members had made. Bringing diversity into the service brought more funding for crews up and down the country, helping us to do even more lifesaving work. We've been visible to the girls like my younger self, who watch lifeboats going out and dream of being on board.

They know that if we can do it, so can they.

People ask what I'll do after I retire fully, but I doubt they'll ever get rid of me. Once my time is up, I plan to be the old fart in the station, drinking tea and telling my stories to the next lot coming through.

That will make me happy indeed.

10.

MAYDAY AT THE HARBOUR'S MOUTH

Dean Hegarty, Castletownbere 2018

I'd only been over at the local shop a few minutes when my pager started to beep. It was around seven o'clock in the evening and I'd just left RNLI Castletownbere Lifeboat Station to grab myself some dinner.

I looked at my pager.

Launch ALB.

It was a request to launch our all-weather lifeboat. Although I was only twenty-four years old, I'd been a volunteer on the crew at the station for five years and I'd recently been appointed as full-time coxswain. This would be my second-ever shout in the position.

I ran straight back over to the station.

It was a terrible night. The winds were gusting storm force 9, even touching 10 at times. Whatever the shout was, I knew it was going to be a tough one.

I was only about fifty metres from the boathouse, so I was the first one to get there, but I knew other crew members would already be on their way. I met Michael Martin-Sullivan, the deputy launching authority, who had more information about the shout.

'What's the story?' I asked.

'It's a mayday,' he said. 'A fishing boat in trouble outside the mouth of the harbour.'

A knot tightened in my stomach.

A mayday.

It was the most urgent of all distress calls, used to signal a life-threatening emergency. It wasn't used lightly.

What's more, I was born and raised in the town, and had worked on fishing boats since I'd left school. I knew exactly where the boat had got into trouble.

The Piper's Rocks.

They were renowned in Castletown Berehaven, to give our town its full title. As the name suggested, the harbour here was calm and sheltered. On a good day it was glorious. But once you got outside of the narrow harbour's mouth, you were out in the Atlantic Ocean and completely exposed. The Piper's were located just to the west of the harbour's mouth. Even in favourable conditions, it was easy for boats to find themselves in difficulty there.

The fishing boat was only two miles from the lifeboat station, but there was no doubt in my mind. Anyone in trouble at the Piper's, in those conditions, was in real danger. If we didn't get out there fast, then the crew of the stricken vessel would be lost.

Like others before them …

Just like many other fishing communities, Castletownbere had seen its share of tragedies out at sea.

Life revolved around the crews taking fishing vessels, trawlers and tugs in and out of the harbour. The RNLI was a vital part of the community, and you came across crew members all the time.

Growing up, my next-door neighbour, Brian O'Driscoll, and the principal of my primary school, Paul Stevens, had both been coxswains on the lifeboat at Castletownbere.

The crew, shore team and fundraising volunteers were well known and respected by everyone. Especially the fundraisers, because they were the reason we had a lifeboat at all.

I was too young to remember it, but the town only got a lifeboat in 1997. The RNLI lifeboat station was officially established the following year, when I was just four years old. Apparently, hundreds had turned out and packed the pier to celebrate the arrival of the Arun class all-weather lifeboat, *The Roy and Barbara Harding*.

There was a good reason for the excitement.

It had taken almost three decades of campaigning, fundraising and persistence from the local community to bring the RNLI to the town.

As a child, I'd been told that it all started in December 1968. A fishing boat had left from nearby Kilmacalogue Harbour in Kenmare Bay to return to Castletownbere's more sheltered harbour for the Christmas break.

Shortly after they left, the weather broke and the wind picked up to a strong gale force, so the trawler had no choice but to turn back towards Kilmacalogue. In awful weather conditions, with pounding rain, the boat had ended up on the rocks.

They'd put out a distress call and RNLI Valentia Lifeboat Station, thirty-five nautical miles north had launched its Watson class lifeboat immediately. But lifeboats were slower at the time and the RNLI's modern navigation technology was yet to be invented. By the time they arrived, it was too late. The boat was already breaking up and all five of its crew members had been lost. In the wake of the tragedy, there were calls for a lifeboat in Castletownbere. Among the people involved was a local lady called Sheila O'Driscoll, who brought the people of the town together.

'Something must be done,' she'd said. 'We need a lifeboat here.'

The close-knit community was in agreement.

However, we had two lifeboat stations nearby: RNLI Valentia Lifeboat Station and RNLI Baltimore Lifeboat Station, about thirty nautical miles south-east of Castletownbere. The RNLI felt the area was well covered and weren't convinced of the need for another lifeboat in the area. But they had another question for Sheila and her supporters as well.

How will you pay for the lifeboat?

Because the RNLI was a charity, they didn't have the funds to just give a town a lifeboat. Money needed to be raised to buy an RNLI vessel and equip its crew.

And that didn't come cheap.

Sheila already knew that, though. She and the local community rose to the challenge, arranging all sorts of fundraising activities.

Fashion shows, dinner dances, lotto, sponsored haircuts, head shaves and moustache removal …

From what my older relatives told me, if you could name it, they'd done it, all in the name of raising money for the town's own lifeboat.

Everyone always gave generously, especially the fishing community. The people of the town and the RNLI worked together to help make a lifeboat station for Castletownbere a reality.

It was the treacherous nature of the harbour mouth and the vast exposed seas that made getting a lifeboat so important for Castletownbere. If vessels got into trouble near the Piper's Rocks or any of the rocky shores near the harbour, they needed assistance in minutes, not hours.

Tragedy had revisited the community in 1986, when a Spanish trawler got into trouble just outside the harbour and found herself lashed against the Piper's Rocks. The boat had been opened up like a sardine can by the perilous outcrop and all five crew members were lost.

Perished at sea.

Being a fishing community and working in unpredictable waters often went hand in hand with tragedy. But the people of the town knew that some of those tragedies could perhaps have been avoided.

If only Castletownbere had its own lifeboat.

Thankfully, the town and the RNLI never gave up. Despite setbacks and problems, eventually we had our lifeboat.

By the time I started working on fishing boats myself at the age of fifteen, I was well aware of the role that the RNLI played in our community. It sounds strange, but even as a fisherman who spent his life out on the water, I always feared the sea. I could check and recheck my forecasts, but you never really knew what it was going to do. It was unpredictable and dangerous at the best of times.

If you were out there in bad weather, it was a crazy place.

It always made me think about the RNLI and how they would be there if we needed them. I had the skills and local knowledge, so it made sense to volunteer as well.

I wanted to give something back to my community.

I was nervous when I joined. A few years earlier, the Arun-class lifeboat had been replaced with a brand new state-of-the-art Severn class all-weather lifeboat, so there was a lot to learn. I was also much younger than many of the crew, but they all welcomed me with open arms. Brian, who'd been my next-door neighbour when I was a child, was coxswain at the time too.

'I'll help you through your training,' he said.

And he did.

It didn't take long for me to feel like I'd always been part of the crew.

Three years after joining as a volunteer, I was working as a skipper of a fish-farm well-boat – a vessel that could transport live fish – out of a place in Donegal, eight and a half hours away from Castletownbere. It was a good job, but the travelling was tough and all my friends were back in my hometown.

I wanted nothing more than to find a job on my doorstep.

So when I spotted an advert for the position of coxswain at Castletownbere on the RNLI website, I didn't hesitate. I knew I was young to be a coxswain, but I had lots of experience from working as a skipper on the salmon-farm boats. I was used to manoeuvring big vessels in tricky seas and I was already a volunteer crew member.

It was worth a try.

I filled in the application, and was called for my first ever job interview in Galway a few weeks later.

Well, you didn't interview to go fishing, did you?

It was nerve-wracking, but I gave it my best shot.

The next day, my phone rang.

'You've got the job,' the RNLI representative said.

'That's brilliant. Thank you,' I said.

To say I was delighted would be an understatement.

Finally, I'd be working out of the town I loved, near to my friends and family and supporting my local community, full-time. What's more, I'd be working alongside a superb crew that had masses of experience I could learn from, and who I knew would support me ferociously.

It was that knowledge that steeled me as we powered out on my second shout as RNLI Castletownbere's coxswain, just five weeks after I'd got the job.

I listened intently as Michael relayed the information from the coastguard. Six fishermen had found themselves adrift in a twenty-five-metre fishing boat after it had suffered a fouled propeller. One of their ropes had been trailing and got caught up in it.

They'd lost power and were now being battered by the south-easterly gale-force nine winds, which were pushing them towards the deadly shoreline near the Piper's Rocks at the entrance to the harbour.

'The vessel that's in trouble is the *Clodagh O,*' he said.

I gasped. The *Clodagh O* was a boat I'd worked on for a couple of weeks in the past. I knew the skipper and his crew really well. They were a capable crew, but in these conditions it wasn't about experience or ability. With a fouled propeller and without power to drive the boat away from those rocks, you were at the mercy of the elements.

Without our assistance, there was only one outcome.

I wasn't going to let that happen on my watch.

Moments after my chat with the deputy launching authority, Marney O'Donoghue – our full-time mechanic – arrived. We usually launched with seven crew members, but not tonight.

Tonight was different.

'Get the boat started straight away,' I said to Marney. 'We have a mayday.'

'OK,' he said, grabbing his kit as he passed.

John Paul Downey and Dave Fenton were the next two to arrive at the station. John Paul was a local painter and decorator who'd been a volunteer crew member for many years. Despite not working at sea, he was from a family of commercial fishermen and had fished for mackerel with his grandfather as a young lad. Like me, he'd joined to give something back to the community.

Dave had moved to Castletownbere after he'd met his wife. His family were also fishermen and boatbuilders. He worked as a local Garda – an Irish police officer – in the town, but it was his family's work at sea that led him to volunteering on the lifeboat.

The pair of them grabbed their kit and ran to the lifeboat as they realised the urgency of the shout. I looked at the clock on the wall. Only a couple of minutes had passed, but I knew we were running out of time.

Seven crew was the norm, but five was the minimum.

Right now I had four, including myself.

I made a decision.

We couldn't wait for seven. We'd launch with the next crew member that walked through the door.

We had to.

I turned to Michael Martin-Sullivan, the deputy launching authority.

'I think we need to launch with five crew,' I said.

'I agree. There's no time to lose,' he said.

With that, I grabbed another set of waterproofs and a life-jacket, and stood in the boathouse. It must have been seconds before Seamus Harrington, a local shipping agent from Castletownbere and volunteer crew member, burst through the door, but it felt like an eternity.

I held his gear out to him.

'Get kitted up on board,' I said. 'We're launching now.'

I could already hear the boat's engine as we ran down to the gangway, pulling on our lifejackets as we went. Seamus and I climbed on board, to find the other crew members all in position and ready to go.

Marney and John Paul were in the wheelhouse, while Dave was out on deck. After starting up the boat, Marney had taken up position as radio operator, to maintain communications with the lifeboat station and the coastguard. John Paul, an experienced navigator, had taken his place at the chart table.

'Get the radar up and put her position in,' I said to John Paul.

'ETA three minutes,' he said.

With the radar up and our route plotted, John Paul was free to head up on deck to help Dave, while I took the helm.

We launched in record time. Just six minutes after the mayday call had come in.

'When we get to them, we'll have to establish a tow – and fast,' I said to the crew.

'I'll get the tow ready,' Dave said.

But even before I'd said it, Dave was already on his way to get the heaving line. Once again, I felt a sense of reassurance. I was going out with a very capable crew.

They all knew exactly what they were doing.

And they knew how serious it was too.

There was no room for hesitation or error. As much as I had total confidence in the ability of my crew, my stomach still churned with nerves as we powered out of the harbour. All we had was the information that the deputy launching authority had given me.

She was adrift with no power.

But that information was minutes old. Out at the harbour mouth, everything could have changed by the time we got there.

Had they run aground? Had they abandoned ship? Would we get there in time?

What's more, I could feel responsibility weighing on me. Not just for the six fishermen on the *Clodagh O*, but for the four men on my crew. I was only twenty-four, with no wife or children. They had families that they needed to get home to. The crew were volunteers, risking their lives and asking nothing in return.

It was my duty to bring them home safely.

And then there was the boat, the *Annette Hutton*, a three-million-euro vessel that protected our town and fishing community. She needed to come back safely too.

I headed into the weather, steaming out as fast as we could, with the spray from the waves and heavy rain soaking us. We hadn't even had time to put our waterproof jackets on.

Eyes on the harbour mouth, I gripped the wheel and took a deep breath. I was nervous but determined.

We were going to bring them all home.

Within ten minutes of the original mayday call, we were on the scene. I won't lie about my reaction to what I saw when we arrived – it almost gave me a heart attack.

The way the tide was going out and the wind was coming in, it was churning up the sea and creating enormous watery explosions. There were huge swells reaching six metres, the height of a two-storey house, tossing the fishing boat around like a rag doll and pushing her ever closer to the sixty-metre cliffs to the west of the harbour mouth.

The gales were now peaking at storm force 11.

My heart started to race as I watched the waves crashing up

against the cliffs, with the vessel only thirty or so metres away from the rocky shoreline.

I could see the skipper in the wheelhouse and the five crew members assembled on deck at the bow of the boat. As we'd bounced out of the harbour, Marney had communicated our plan to the stricken boat's crew using the VHF radio.

They were ready.

I glanced at my crew working on deck. The tow was already lying ready across the deck and the heaving line was attached.

My crew were ready too.

Eyeing the waves rolling in against the *Clodagh O* and taking note of the force of impact and the distance they were pushing the boat each time, I knew that we had only one chance here.

One chance to pass the line over.

One chance to establish the tow.

One chance to save those six lives.

'I'm coming alongside her,' I said, as I carefully manoeuvred the lifeboat towards the *Clodagh O*. As I did, I saw Dave grab the heaving line and tow, and move into position on our stern.

'I have a line ready to pass,' he shouted.

'OK,' came the reply from the *Clodagh O*.

'Put the tow rope over the first cleat you can and we'll get you out of there,' Dave roared.

Then he picked up the heaving line and stood primed to launch it, waiting for the moment when we were as close as I could safely get us without colliding with the fishing boat. Steering carefully, I managed to get about ten metres from her.

'That's as close as I can go,' I shouted over the howling wind.

'OK,' Dave replied.

I held my breath as I watched him pull his arm back and launch the heaving line towards the *Clodagh O* with as much force as he physically could.

He gave it absolutely everything he had.

This had to work. If it didn't, there was no other option, no Plan B. The *Clodagh O* was now about fifteen metres away from the deadly rocks and moments from being lost.

It felt like time stood still as the line sailed through the air.

Please let them grab it.

After what felt like an eternity, the tow landed on the deck of the *Clodagh O*. Within a second, the crew had grabbed it and secured it to the nearest cleat, just like Dave had told them to.

Yes!

We'd done it. Against all the odds.

Suddenly, everything sped up again.

'Lock off the tow rope,' I shouted to Dave, who reacted immediately.

It was just as well too.

As I prepared to bring the boat around, two gigantic waves rolled through. My jaw swung open as I shook my head in disbelief as the first launched the *Clodagh O* clean out of the water.

We'd got hold of them in the nick of time.

If we hadn't attached the tow when we did, they'd be gone now.

The second wave would have made sure of that.

249

We'd been lucky, but the job wasn't over. We still needed to get *Clodagh O* away from the violent swell she was in and back into the shelter of the harbour. As tempting as it was to go full throttle and get out of there as fast as we could, I knew that to do so would easily part the tow.

Gale-force winds were still screaming around us, and both our lifeboat and the *Clodagh O* were being tossed around in the mountainous seas.

If we lost the boat here, we'd never get her back.

And six lives were dangling on that tow line.

It was going to take care and patience to return them all back home safely. After getting us this far, I wasn't taking any chances.

I gently turned the lifeboat around and brought the bow into the weather, leaving her in gear and heading back towards the shelter of the harbour at about half a knot.

That way, we kept a loose tow.

It took us forty-five minutes to travel about a quarter of a mile, but at least it meant she stayed with us.

But she still wasn't out of trouble yet.

In the short time we'd been out, the weather conditions had deteriorated. There was still a massive swell, and the fishing boat was bouncing up and down on our tow. Every wave threatened to part the line and sweep her away.

Thankfully, two tugboats close by had offered their assistance after hearing the mayday. One had been carrying divers in the harbour, the other was piloting a Spanish fishing boat into the harbour. It was typical of the seafaring community, always looking out for one another.

'They're going to stand by inside the harbour just in case anything goes wrong,' Marney said.

'Great,' I said.

We were nearly home, but we still needed all the help we could get.

Eventually, flanked by the two tugboats, we pulled up alongside the pier and were able to get the stricken fishing boat berthed safely.

When we were all safely back inside the station, the skipper came up to me.

'Thank you,' he said. 'Thank you so much.'

'You're welcome. You did the right thing putting out a mayday straight away,' I said. 'Especially in these conditions.'

Truth be told, it felt like a lot of very good split-second decisions had been made by everyone involved that night. From the skipper's mayday, to our decision to launch with five men and Dave prepping the tow as soon as we were on our way.

Precision, quick thinking and teamwork had saved those lives.

Once the lifeboat was washed down and made ready for service again, I still had one more task to complete as coxswain.

The return-of-service report was a form that the coxswain needed to fill in after each shout. In it, he had to explain what had just happened, so that the RNLI could review the operation and make sure that all procedures had been properly followed.

I was still new to the job and more accustomed to being hands-on on the lifeboat, but I was already getting used to some of the paperwork. With the shout still fresh in my mind, I sat down and completed the form.

'We launched at 7.30pm. We established a tow and rescued the casualty vessel. We returned to the lifeboat station at 9.30pm,' I wrote.

Done.

The former coxswain and current RNLI area lifesaving manager, Brian O'Driscoll, rang me a few days later.

'You're going to need a bit more detail than that, Dean,' he said, chuckling.

Turns out that the report had to include who did what and what happened when, step by step and in minute detail.

Honestly, I had no idea. But with a little guidance from Brian, I got it done – and it was a fair bit longer than my original three sentences!

It might have been a relatively quick rescue, but for a new coxswain like myself it was a real test of my abilities. The *Clodagh O* had found herself in the worst possible place, in the worst possible conditions and at the worst possible time.

After the rescue, Paul Stevens, our operations manager and press officer, made a statement for local media and the RNLI's media team.

'Time was of the essence this evening, and I would like to commend our volunteer crew for the fast response that had them on scene and providing help within ten minutes of the mayday,' he said. 'Given the weather conditions and how close the fishing boat was drifting to the shore at this point, the lifeboat's timely arrival avoided a potential tragedy.'

I agreed with every word.

It was a fantastic feeling to have brought not only all six of the *Clodagh O*'s crew members home safely to their families, but the boat too. It was their livelihood, after all.

I felt like I'd done a good job, but more than anything I was proud of what my crew had achieved. I hadn't needed to tell them anything – they knew exactly what to do. They were a well-oiled machine that I'd been honoured to command.

It was over a year later when we found out that the rescue had been considered by the RNLI's medals committee. I was stunned to find out that I'd be receiving a Bronze Medal for Gallantry, while Marney, Seamus, John Paul, Dave and Michael Martin-Sullivan were all to receive a framed Letter of Thanks from the chairman of the RNLI.

What's more, it was the first time that anyone from RNLI Castletownbere's crew had been honoured with a medal and the first time in a decade that a medal had been awarded to an RNLI crew member in Ireland.

The last one had been awarded to a mechanic called Anthony Chambers at RNLI Portrush Lifeboat Station [*Race against the tide*, p. 189], who'd fought against a rising tide to rescue two boys from a cave back in 2009.

I've been called brave an awful lot since the RNLI's announcement in January 2020, but I don't think that I am. I'm just doing my job.

It's a job I couldn't do without my crew.

To me, it's them who are brave. They are the heroes in my eyes.

Whether it had been the same four guys or other members of our crew that went out that night, I know it would have worked out the same.

I might be biased, but we really do have the very best at RNLI Castletownbere.

It's hard to put into words what we have here, what got us through that night. But Sheila – our former fundraising secretary and one of the reasons we have our lifeboat – explains it better than I ever could.

We have a great crew. A crew that can trust their coxswain and a coxswain that can trust his crew.

I'm not the reason six lives were saved that night.

We are.

Crew, shore support, fundraisers and the town that supports us.

We did it together.

11.

TRAPPED BY THE TIDE

Vicky Murphy, St Agnes 2009

It was just the same way we'd spent many Sundays in the year since we'd started dating – a beautiful sunny afternoon strolling along the sands of Chapel Porth beach in St Agnes in our welly boots. Clasping hands, my boyfriend Marc and I wound left around the headland towards Wheal Charlotte, a secluded cove just a few minutes' walk away.

Waddling along at thirty-five weeks pregnant, I knew there probably weren't many weekends left when I'd be able to manage the walk, so I soaked it all up. The warm rays of the sun and gentle breeze danced across my face as we plodded along, talking excitedly about becoming parents. It was our first baby together.

'I can't wait to know what we're having,' I said to Marc.

'I know,' he smiled.

We both thought it would be a boy, but as long as it was healthy we really didn't mind. It was the start of a whole new chapter for us. We'd been friends for eight years, but around a year earlier we'd both come out of long-term relationships.

We'd turned to one another for support and before we knew it, we were a couple.

We'd set up home where we met, in Swanscombe in Kent, but once the baby made an appearance and we were settled into parenthood, we planned to move down to Cornwall for a fresh start as a family.

By the time we reached Wheal Charlotte, I was already starting to feel tired. I dropped the carrier bag full of bananas that I'd been carrying and sat down on the sand. I gazed out towards the sea and Marc sat beside me, while we chatted about decorating the nursery and getting my hospital bag ready in the coming weeks. Then a wave of drowsiness washed over me. I stretched and lay back on the sand.

'I might have a rest here for a bit,' I said.

'OK,' he said, planting a kiss on my forehead. 'I'm going to have a look over there.'

As I watched him pad away to explore some nearby rocks, I felt my eyes starting to droop. Basking in the sunshine, cocooned by its warmth and relaxed by the sound of the waves in the distance, I started to daydream.

This is perfect.

Chapel Porth beach had always had a special place in my heart. It was where my dad, Ray, had often visited in his younger years and he'd turned it into our family tradition. He and my mum, Sharon, would pile me, my big brother Dean and my little sister Rachael into his Ford Capri to make the four-and-a-half-hour journey from our home in Surrey to St Agnes.

We'd stay in a little cottage at the top of the road that wound down to Chapel Porth beach. Each day we'd walk down and play together, tuck into pasties from the pasty hut and dip our toes in the shallow water on the shoreline, until the tide started to come in.

I loved it there, but you'd never catch me swimming in the sea. Not because I couldn't, but because I didn't want to. You see, despite all our great memories, I had a recurring nightmare that kept me from venturing any further than ankle-deep into the water.

As a little girl, the dream would always be the same. I'd be on Chapel Porth beach, playing inside one of the caves along the cliffs. Suddenly, the tide would start to come in. The water would be rising fast, swirling round, and I'd start to panic. I'd be skirting around the walls of a cave, trying to climb up and out of an opening at the top. All the while, I'd be being chased.

By a whale, running along on its back fins.

It was daft, really, the product of a child's overactive imagination and maybe a few too many cartoons. But it still had me waking up in a cold sweat.

Spending time at the coast, my mum and dad had always taught us to respect the sea. None of us were big swimmers or surfers, like other people we saw down there, but watching the RNLI lifeguards on the beach and seeing the charity's orange lifeboats bouncing out on the waves was always a reminder of how easy it was to get into trouble at sea.

We knew they did an important job, so we always put a few coins in the pot if they were fundraising and we always behaved sensibly.

I continued having the dream into adulthood. By then the whale running on its fins had stopped making an appearance, but I was always in a cave.

And always on Chapel Porth beach.

That said, I never let it stop me from going there. When Marc and I started dating, it didn't take me long to suggest making the trip for a date. The opportunity to create even more precious memories there far outweighed one silly nightmare for me.

Suddenly, I felt a hand gently nudging my shoulder and my attention snapped back to the beach.

I must have dozed off, I thought, as my eyes fluttered open. I blinked a few times and Marc's face came into focus.

'Come on, sweetheart,' he said. 'We'd better start making our way back round the headlands. The tide's starting to push in.'

'How long was I asleep?' I asked.

'Not long. Fifteen minutes or so,' he said, holding out his hand to help me up. I grabbed it and planted my other hand in the sand, pushing myself up so I could get back on my feet.

I could have stayed there all day, but he was right. The tide looked miles out from where I was standing, but it was better to be safe.

'Let's get going then,' I sighed, brushing sand off my denim maternity dungarees and picking up the plastic bag.

Retracing our path back to Chapel Porth beach, we began to make our way back to the headland. I rubbed my bump protectively as we ambled hand in hand, without a care in the world. It was quiet and peaceful, and I couldn't help but think how lovely it would be to be able to do this walk all the time. Me, Marc and our new baby.

I can't wait to move here, I thought.

It only took us a few minutes to walk to the edge of the cove. I knew that once we turned that corner, the headland would come into view and we'd almost be back at the beach. I wasn't paying all that much attention as we came out of the cove, until Marc stopped in his tracks. I instantly knew something wasn't right.

'What's up?' I asked.

'Look at that,' he said, pointing towards the headland. I followed his finger and then gasped out loud.

'The tide's already right in,' he said, before I could say anything.

'But how …?' I trailed off.

We'd only been in the cove for about half an hour. Last time we'd seen the headland the tide had been miles out. Even when we left the cove it hadn't looked like it was anywhere near shore.

We should have had plenty of time to get back, I thought.

Yet, here we were, staring open-mouthed as the waves splashed at the base of the cliffs in the distance.

'We'd better get a move on,' Marc said.

'OK,' I said.

But it was easier said than done at thirty-five weeks pregnant. We continued our slow stroll back towards Chapel Porth beach. It was all I could manage. The water was lapping around our feet and ankles, but I figured that if we kept up the steady pace we'd make it round just fine. After all, the tide had only just started to come in. There was no way it could cut us off that quickly.

Could it?

Minutes later, I had my answer. I was five foot tall and the water was already up to my shins. Another few minutes passed and it was at my knees, trickling into my wellies.

My heart started to race. I'd never known a tide come in so fast.

But then, I never swam in the sea.

Suddenly, I became aware that I wasn't walking anymore.

I was wading.

'Sweetheart, you're going to have to move a bit faster,' Marc said suddenly, his brow creased.

He looked worried.

'I'm trying,' I said, indicating my protruding bump and raising my eyebrows in an exasperated manner. Not only was I almost full term, I'd carried heavy as well. It was hard enough just to walk, let alone wade through waves with wet denim dungarees dragging me down.

'I know,' he said, grabbing my hand tightly. 'But we've still got quite a way to get around.'

Walking along earlier, it had only taken us ten minutes, but now even a few feet was taking us minutes rather than seconds to get through.

We moved in silence. By now I could feel the water inching up my leg. Each time it crept higher, it became more difficult for me to move.

It was like wading through treacle.

'Come on, sweetheart,' Marc urged. 'You need to move faster.'

'I can't,' I said, biting my lip to fight back tears.

'You have to,' he pleaded.

He couldn't disguise the panic in his voice now. Looking at the cliffs ahead and the waves rolling in, my heart was pounding. My whole body started to shake and I stopped dead in my tracks. I grabbed Marc, spun him around and looked him straight in the eye.

'Be honest with me,' I said to him. 'We're not going to make it back round there, are we?'

Inside I was praying that he'd laugh it off. Tell me to stop being silly and say something reassuring. Instead he was silent, his face completely still and staring me dead in the eye.

'No,' he said.

With that single word, my whole world came crashing down.

Within minutes of Marc confirming my worst fear, the water was up at my chest. His green hoodie was drenched and weighing him down, so he took it off. I dumped the bag full of bananas too. There was no point lugging them along anymore.

Any extra weight was just slowing us down.

I felt sick as I saw the force with which the waves wrenched our belongings away. Gripping onto Marc, I shook my head frantically and started gasping for breath as panic gripped me. I was scared.

For me. For Marc.

And the baby …

'What do we do?' I said. 'Should we go back to the cove?'

Marc shook his head as he looked back at where we'd come from. Water was closing in on us from both sides.

'Well, what? Do we carry on walking?' I said, throwing my hands up. 'Or do we just wait for the water to get us?'

Marc put his hands on my shoulders.

'It's quicker to carry on than walk back,' Marc said. 'We just have to keep going and see if we can get around.'

If ...

Silently, we tried to move forward, but we were pushing against a tide that was now running in at full force. Marc had looped his arm through the straps of my dungarees at the back, to keep hold of me. But the waves were getting stronger and stronger.

Before we knew it, I was shoulder deep and we'd been pushed up against a cliff wall. Waves were crashing all around us, getting higher and stronger with every moment.

Goodness knows how, but Marc managed to dig his wellies into the ground beneath the water to hold himself still. He grabbed hold of a protruding rock and with his spare arm was holding onto me.

There was no way now for us to move anywhere.

We were stuck.

Or at least Marc was.

With the waves now almost five feet high, I was on tiptoes and struggling to keep my head above water. Suddenly, I felt something beneath me, pulling at my body and whipping me clean off my feet.

I screamed.

'Marc, keep hold of me!' I yelled. Immediately, I felt the straps of my dungarees go taut as the water dragged me away from Marc.

'What is it?' he said, pulling me back towards him.

'It's a rip current,' I said.

You didn't need to be a swimmer or a diver to know.

The rip was stronger than I could fight. My feet off the ground I was now being tossed horizontally around by the waves. As it retreated I lowered back to the floor, only for it to come back stronger and harder. This time it whipped my welly boots right off my feet, carrying them away with the tide.

I screamed again and my stomach churned. If Marc didn't keep hold of those straps. I'd be dragged away and I'd drown.

And if I drowned?

So would our baby …

Our baby. It was all I could think about. As the waves tossed me around, I tried to clasp my arms protectively around my bump, but it was futile. Every wave that came threw me violently against the cliff face and against the jagged rocks. I was freezing from being immersed in the water for so long, but I could still feel the cuts and bruises throbbing.

Our poor baby …

Shivering and sobbing, I was helpless to protect it.

Looking ahead of us, out to sea, there were waves climbing to five feet tall. They were heading straight for us and there was nothing we could do.

Except wait …

The wave crept closer and closer, until it was towering above us, about to break. We both sucked in a big breath and then …

CRASSSHHHHHHH.

The wave collided on top of us, submerging us in angry, confused seas. Marc held onto me for what felt like hours until it finally pulled away from us.

'Oh my God,' I gasped.

But we only had a few moments' respite.

Over and over the waves came in. Over and over they crashed down on us. Relentless and always climbing.

I didn't know how long I'd be able to take it. Or how long Marc would be able to hold on for.

Thoughts started to spin through my mind. Did anyone know we were here? Had anyone seen us when we were struggling to get back? Perhaps someone had alerted the coastguard?

If they had, wouldn't help be here by now?

Looking out to sea, I saw nothing. No boats, no people. Just a huge six-foot wave ploughing right towards us. It was the biggest we'd seen so far.

In blind panic I looked up at Marc. He'd seen it too.

Was he going to be able to hold onto me?

It was huge, and I knew that it was going to completely engulf me. I craned my neck to look back up at Marc through the surf and spray.

'Keep hold of me,' I pleaded.

But he didn't say anything. He just stared straight down at me. His eyes were filled with desperation.

In that moment I knew what his haunted look meant. It was saying the unsayable.

I can't hold onto you.

No matter how much he wanted to, I could tell he just couldn't do it anymore.

'No, please,' I sobbed as the wave loomed above us.

I looked at him one last time. He was still staring at me in desperation. A shiver ran down my spine.

Please keep hold. Then I sucked in a deep breath.

The wave crashed down, the impact pushing me deep into the water. I was plunged into darkness. The sound of churning water enveloped me and I felt myself being tossed around violently.

It was like being stuck in a washing machine.

I'd probably only been submerged for a few moments, but I felt like I was underwater for an eternity. I'd been spun in so many different directions that I had no idea if I was still upright.

Or if Marc still had hold of me …

Finally I resurfaced, coughing and gasping for breath, with water and hair in my eyes.

But as my vision readjusted and I regained my bearings, my heart leapt. Marc was still there, clinging onto the boulder. His arm still wrapped around my dungaree straps.

He still had hold of me.

It was a fleeting moment of relief. But just as soon as the wave had pulled away, another was on its way. The sea was like a hammer, intent on chipping us away.

How many more blows could he take?

Even if he kept hold of me, would he be able to hold onto the rock? I had no idea how long we'd been there, but Marc had been clinging on the whole time. He only had so much strength.

It was only a matter of time, I thought.

And I was right. When the next wave crashed down on us, I felt myself dragged and tossed around in new directions. The wave had torn Marc's hand away from the rock we'd been anchored to.

Submerged in the salty waves, I suddenly thought, *This is it.*

So I closed my eyes.

But it wasn't over yet. Once again I burst through the surface of the waves, gulping for air. Nearby, Marc was doing the same. Detached from the boulder, we were being smashed up against the cliff face and into one another with every wave that came in. Each minute seemed to stretch into infinity as all the fight drained from my body.

I can't do it anymore. I can't do it.

I was ready for the waves to take me. To make it all be over.

I was ready to give up.

But then, as the wave pulled out, I felt myself being shoved up onto a new rock. Solid ground within my grasp, I began to scramble up instinctively, wriggling along on my bulbous belly.

What the …?

From being caught up in the swell, I was suddenly sitting on a cliff base, with rocks all around me, just out of the reach of the waves. I turned and saw Marc. He was next to me, but not as high up as I was.

It was then that I realised what had happened. We'd been tossed towards a gully in the cliffs, like a small cave. When the wave had gone out, Marc had seen an opportunity and gathered all his strength to shove me up onto the cliff base.

But he'd not made it up himself.

'Marc,' I screamed, desperately.

But he didn't move, he was just lying down, lifeless, like he was just waiting for the next wave to take him.

Or like he was already dead.

'No!' I screamed, as I watched the next wave bowling in. 'Marc!'

But he didn't move.

I leaned over slightly and allowed another scream to tear from my throat.

'Marc, get up. Get up,' I screamed through tears. 'Don't leave me!'

Suddenly, he moved.

'Get up here,' I shouted, eyes darting rapidly between Marc and the wave that was roaring in.

What happened next, I have no idea. But one minute, Marc was lying helplessly beneath me.

And the next?

He was back beside me.

We scrambled as far back along the cliff base as we could and stood up, clinging onto one another. For a moment we were silent. Looking around, there wasn't another soul to be seen.

There was nothing more than a matter of feet between us and the still-rising tide, either.

Reality collapsed on top of me like a tonne of bricks. No one had seen us. No one was coming to get us. Within minutes, we'd be back in the water.

We're as good as dead.

Suddenly, all my panic turned into what felt like calmness. I didn't realise it then, but shock was setting in. I turned to Marc, just like when we'd been wading towards the headland.

'We're not going to make it, are we?' I asked. This time, though, it was a rhetorical question.

Marc knew I knew the answer. We were shivering, battered and bruised. I was heavily pregnant and Marc was exhausted from desperately clinging onto me and whatever he could grab hold of, to stop us from drifting away.

Despite all his efforts, we weren't going to make it. Instead of saying anything, Marc just hugged me tightly.

'I can't believe my mum and dad are going to get this news,' I said, tears pouring down my face. 'Going to find out that our bodies have been washed up on shore.'

Drowned in a place we all loved so much.

Then another thought entered my head.

'I can't believe we're not going to have this baby,' I said, tears streaking my cheeks. We'd waited for almost nine months to meet our baby, wondering about it every day. But we'd never get to meet it. Marc placed his hand on my tummy.

'I wonder if we were having a boy or a girl,' he said. I clasped my hand over his.

'I guess we'll never know,' I said. 'I wonder if they'll tell our parents the sex. After they find our bodies?'

It was a morbid thought, but I genuinely had no idea.

Did they even check that kind of thing if they found a drowned pregnant woman?

It wouldn't matter to us, though. We'd never know.

I turned to Marc.

'We should say our goodbyes,' I said, squeezing his hand. I knew once the waves took us, we'd be torn apart. The water was already lapping over the lip of the rock now. This really was it. Our last chance to say anything that needed to be said.

But where do you even start?

In a second, all our years of friendship flashed before my eyes. Our first date, moving in together and finding out we were expecting. Visions of how excited our parents had been about the news. Memories of my childhood holidays in St Agnes that had led us here today.

I said the only thing I could.

'I love you,' I said, sobbing. 'I've always loved you.'

'I love you too,' Marc replied, before wrapping his arms around me and our precious bump. For a moment, we were silent, locked in our embrace. Then, we untangled ourselves from our hug and turned to look out to sea.

It was still desolate, abandoned.

By now, I'd accepted that we were dead. We were just waiting. Waiting for the wave that would finally wash our family away, taking with it all of our hopes and dreams.

Would it be this one? Or this one?

It didn't matter.

But despite that, despite the fact that I couldn't see a person or boat for miles, I turned towards Chapel Porth beach and started waving. Waving and shouting. As I did, Marc started scrambling around, trying to find a way out or a route over the cliff.

Even though we were resigned to our fate, something pushed us to keep on trying, right up to the bitter end. Maybe it was human nature or the thought of our helpless baby. But we kept trying.

After a few minutes, cold began to grip my body. We'd only been in the water for about twenty-five minutes, but I was soaked to the bone. I was trembling and hypothermia was starting to set in.

Well, if the waves didn't get me …

Standing arms aloft on the cliff base, being lashed by freezing sea spray, I was numb. My head started to swim. I felt like I was trapped in a bubble, like this was all one big dream that I was waiting to wake up from. But I wasn't waking up.

Then, out of nowhere, I saw it. At first I had to rub my eyes to make sure they weren't playing tricks on me. That I wasn't suffering from some kind of delirium. But it was definitely there. Coming around the headland from Porthtowan beach.

A motorboat.

A bright orange motorboat, bouncing through the waves. All my years visiting Chapel Porth beach told me exactly what it was.

It was an RNLI boat!

'Thank goodness!' I exclaimed as I started to wave harder. 'Marc, look!'

'Oh, my goodness,' he said. 'Is that …?'

'HEEEEELLLLLLLPPPP,' I screamed, before he could even finish. I didn't want to risk them missing us, if it wasn't us they were out for.

'Over here! Help!' Marc shouted, jumping and waving.

'My baby!' I yelled. I had no idea why, but I did.

It only took a moment to realise that they were definitely heading straight for us. They'd either *just* seen us or they'd been alerted by someone else. Either way, it didn't matter.

All that mattered was that help was coming.

I crumpled with relief.

We're going to be OK. We're going to be rescued.

Emotion overwhelmed me. My parents wouldn't have to get that heart-breaking call. And we were going to have our baby.

Our baby was going to be OK.

I burst into tears, and hope sent a surge of adrenaline through my body as the boat drew nearer. But suddenly it stopped.

'What's happening?' I thought out loud.

'It's too choppy for them to bring the boat in,' Marc said. We'd been tossed so far from where we'd started that we were stuck in a cave along the cliff face.

'So how will they …?' I began.

Almost on cue, one of the men, dressed in the red and yellow of the RNLI lifeguards and pulling a long buoyant tube, jumped out of the boat and started swimming towards us.

My jaw dropped as he powered through the waves. I'd been in that sea. It amazed me that anyone would get in voluntarily.

And be able to get anywhere in it.

Minutes later, he was at the ledge at the cliff base.

'I'm an RNLI lifeguard,' he said.

Then he looked at me and did a double-take. I realised instantly what was going through his mind.

She's heavily pregnant.

He didn't miss a beat, though.

'I'm going to help you,' he said.

I was nodding at him, too scared to speak, even as his colleague leapt out of the boat as well. He had another long buoyant tube with him as he pushed through the waves towards us. I was stunned. I couldn't believe that anyone would get into this water voluntarily.

For a pair of complete strangers.

'We're going to have to get you into the water,' the lifeguard said, snapping me out of my thoughts.

My stomach lurched and my whole body started to shake. He wanted me to get back in that water? I knew he was a lifeguard, but I was too frightened. I'd been in it once and I didn't want to go back in.

And I certainly didn't want to leave Marc.

'I, I, I can't,' I stuttered.

'You can,' he said patiently.

'I'm not leaving Marc,' I said. 'Please don't make me.'

But before I could protest further, he pulled me down from the ledge, into the water and gave me the long floating tube to hold on to.

'This is a rescue tube,' he said. 'Hold on to it.'

As we started to move through the surf, I was terrified. Just like Marc and I had been earlier, we were tossed all over the place, bouncing off submerged rocks. Ahead of me I could see the other lifeguard, now halfway towards us in the water.

He was being thrown about by the waves too.

I allowed myself to be passed over to him.

'He's going to get you onto the boat,' the first lifeguard said, as his colleague gave me his rescue tube and pulled me steadily back towards the boat.

The incoming tide was rising fast, yet he somehow managed to keep hold of me.

How was he managing it?

272

The next thing I remember is finding myself inside the boat and looking around for Marc.

My heart was in my mouth as I caught sight of the first life-guard swimming with him, the second poised nearby ready to get him in the boat, as he had done me.

They were so close, but the waves were still smashing against the rocks and tossing them all around.

'Get him back,' I muttered, clutching my bump.

Then, almost out of nowhere, a huge wave crashed over Marc and the lifeguard who was with him. I stood up and gasped.

Please come up. I thought, as I waited for the wave to recede.

As it did, my heart sank. They were nowhere to be seen.

'No!' I screamed. I crumpled into a heap on the boat.

It was too much. My whole body was shaking and I felt like my heart was breaking.

I've lost him. I've lost Marc. I thought.

There was just no sign of them. It was like time stood still for me. Everything around me ground to a halt, even the waves seemed to fall silent as anguish enveloped me.

Until suddenly, something incredible happened.

They resurfaced!

Goodness knows exactly what happened. It looked like they'd been pushed backwards into the cave by the wave.

Whatever had occurred, they were out now.

The world sped up again, as the lifeguards dragged Marc onto the boat beside me. Once we were all safely on board, the one who had helped me into the boat took control of the vessel and started driving us back to land.

I was astounded by their bravery. They didn't even pause before coming to get us. As we motored away from the scene, I could clearly see how we'd been battered further and further back, until we were tucked away into a small cave, trapped by the rising tide.

'How did you know we were here?' I wheezed to the lifeguard who was driving the boat.

'We were patrolling Porthtowan beach when a surfer raised the alarm,' he said. 'We spotted you the second time we came past.'

The first time they passed, we must have been under the water.

Thank goodness they came back, I thought.

Not having to concentrate on where the next wave was coming from, my mind started to replay everything that had happened. Then suddenly I brought my hand to my stomach.

'Are you all right?' one of the lifeguards asked, immediately alert to my reaction.

'I haven't felt my baby move,' I said. 'I don't know if it's OK.'

'We've requested an ambulance to shore,' he said. 'They'll check you over.'

But my mind was already running over all the possible scenarios. All the blows my bump had taken against those rocks. The shock of the cold. My own panic. Of course it wouldn't be moving. How could it be?

Then again ...

'But I'm not going to feel it move, am I?' I rationalised. 'I'm in too much shock and panic to feel anything.'

I hung my head and started to cry. Big, heaving sobs that I couldn't control. It was fear and relief all wrapped into one overpowering emotion.

'Let's get you two back,' the lifeguard at the helm said, as he cranked up the speed and we shot off with a roar. As we headed back to shore, I looked at them both again in awe.

They'd just saved our lives.

All three of us.

By the time we approached the headland, the sensation of bouncing on the waves became too much for me and my bump, so they took the decision to ground the boat. From there they dragged the boat the rest of the way around the headland.

Minutes later we were back on Porthtowan beach, the closest place for them to bring us back to shore. All the adrenaline had drained from my body and I couldn't even find the energy to stand up. In the end, they had to carry me out of the boat.

I had an arm around each of the lifeguards and I was hanging there, limp, with not an ounce of energy left in me. Crowds of people were watching as they dragged me along the sand towards the waiting ambulance. Paramedics appeared and wrapped both me and Marc in big foil blankets. I remember doors closing and the sound of sirens. After that, everything was a blur.

The next thing I remember clearly is both of us being in the Royal Cornwall Hospital in Treliske. The first thing I did was call my dad.

'Dad, we're OK,' I said. 'But Marc and I are in hospital in Treliske.'

'What happened?' he said.

'We've been rescued from the sea.'

The line went quiet.

'Dad?' I said. Then I heard a sniffing sound.

He was crying.

'I'm on my way,' he said.

'OK,' I said.

I called my mum, who lived in Hastings, straight after. Just like Dad, she was in bits.

As the nurses buzzed around, checking me over, I replayed the day's events over and over in my mind. We found out that there had been a spring tide that had come in fast and caught us out. It had been awful. Terrifying.

A nightmare.

I shot up in my bed. The whole incident had almost been a frame-by-frame replica of that recurring nightmare I'd had since childhood.

Had those dreams been a premonition?

It was as if I'd always known it was going to happen. Thankfully, though, I'd woken up from this nightmare, like all the rest.

And apart from being bruised, exhausted and suffering from hypothermia, we were fine.

But I still hadn't felt the baby move, so they rushed me to the ultrasound department for an emergency scan. Marc came with me. As the sonographer searched for a heartbeat, we held onto one another, as tightly as we had done on that cliff.

I looked down at my bump, which was covered in red marks, scratches and bruises, then back up at the sonographer.

'Is our baby OK?' I asked, my voice shaking.

Everything was quiet as she ran the scanner over my tummy, searching and searching for a heartbeat.

Please be OK, I thought, over and over.

'Ah ha,' the sonographer said suddenly.

'What?' Marc asked.

She turned and beamed at us both. 'Your baby is just fine. Listen.'

And there it was. The most beautiful sound I'd ever heard.

Ta-tum. Ta-tum. Ta-tum.

It was our baby's heartbeat.

'So there's nothing wrong at all?' I said.

'Count your lucky stars. Your baby's head is engaged. It's down near the birth canal. It will have been protected from all those blows.'

'Thank you,' I sobbed, as Marc clung onto my hand.

Five hours later, Dad arrived with my sister Rachael. He burst into the ward, ran straight over to me and grabbed tight hold of me. For the umpteenth time that day I burst into tears.

'The baby is OK,' I told him.

He couldn't even speak. But I knew how much seeing us safe and well meant to him.

The doctors were worried that the shock of the incident would send me into early labour, so they monitored me and the baby closely for three days before we were allowed home to Swanscombe. Sixteen days later, my waters broke in bed.

All over Marc's legs.

We rushed to Darent Valley Hospital and were taken into the maternity ward. A nurse came to see us. She looked at my chart, then looked up at me.

'Is this your first?' she said.

I nodded.

'Hmm,' she said. 'First babies are usually late.'

Oh no …, I thought.

A lump rose in my throat. And before I could stop myself, I told her all about what had happened two weeks earlier. She looked gobsmacked.

'Well, that could have something to do with it,' she said. 'But everything looks fine, so don't worry.'

I was in hospital for two days before they induced me. Then, finally, at 5.07am on 15 June 2009, Rae Murphy finally made her appearance in the world, weighing a healthy seven pounds.

'Here's your daughter,' the midwife said, passing her over and putting her on my chest.

Our little girl.

The love I felt was indescribable. She was our little miracle.

'We thought we'd lost you,' I sobbed. 'I can't believe that we've got you.'

Yet there she was. Tiny, perfect and all in one piece.

'We'll have to take her to meet the lifeguards who saved us,' I said to Marc.

'Definitely,' he smiled, gazing at us both adoringly.

She wouldn't have been here without them. None of us would.

Rae was about six weeks old when we finally took her to the RNLI lifeguard unit on Porthtowan beach. The local media had already covered the story of our dramatic rescue; in fact, we'd even made headlines in the *West Briton* newspaper.

Heavily pregnant woman cheats death on rocks.

The lifeguards who'd saved us were called Damian Prisk and Chris Lowry. When we decided to visit, we knew the media would probably get wind of it. And rightly so. I wanted the whole world to know just how amazing the RNLI lifeguards were, not to mention how grateful we were.

We turned up armed with a huge tin of biscuits, and I wished we could have taken more. But starting a new family and preparing to move houses meant that money was tight. The boys didn't mind, though. They were just smitten with Rae.

'She's beautiful,' said Chris. 'Congratulations.'

'It's so good to see you safe and well,' said Damian. 'Rae is very cute!'

'She's only here because of you two,' I said. 'Thank you for saving my family.'

I'd wanted to thank the surfer who had spotted us too, but no one had been able to track her down. We owed our family's life to her too.

When the lifeguards had returned from their unsuccessful first sweep of the cliff faces, she'd insisted that they go back out.

We had our photos taken together, then Damian and Chris gave us a teddy, signed by them both, to give to Rae when she was older.

'Thank you,' I said, tears pricking my eyes.

No matter how many times I said it, it never felt like enough.

For every day that passed, we had them to thank. We moved to Cornwall in December 2009 and started our new life away from Kent, just like we'd planned. In 2011, our second child arrived, a gorgeous bouncing baby boy called Dillon. Despite everything, we still went back to Chapel Porth beach as a family. At first it made us nervous, but we were determined to replace the memories of that day with happy ones, just like the ones I'd had there with my parents and siblings.

After moving down, we even visited the beach every Christmas morning. Locals would gather together to have mulled wine and mince pies. It became a family tradition. Then in 2012, Marc did something that made our Christmas morning even more special. We were walking along the beach, Rae toddling on the sand and Dillon in my arms. Suddenly, Marc stopped and dropped to one knee. I gasped as he held out a box containing a ring – a gold band with a sparkling solitaire diamond.

'Vicky, you are my best friend, my soulmate and the love of my life,' he said. 'Will you marry me?'

'Yes!' I exclaimed immediately.

'I love you,' he said, slipping the ring on my finger and kissing me.

A year later we got married in a country pub called the Smugglers Den Inn in Cubert. Rae was our flower girl and Dillon our page boy. It was a small affair, with just close family and friends.

Exactly what we wanted.

When it came to the father-of-the-bride speech, my dad made a very special toast. After briefly telling the story of our rescue, he asked all of our guests to stand and raise their glasses.

'To RNLI lifeguards Chris Lowry and Damian Prisk and the wonderful surfer who raised the alarm. Without them I wouldn't have my daughter, son-in-law or my two beautiful grandchildren. There aren't enough words for me to show the gratitude I feel towards them. Cheers!'

'Cheers!' our guests echoed, followed by whoops and shouts of joy. It was a truly special moment.

In the years that followed, we welcomed another member into our brood. Our son Tristan was born in 2014 – another little miracle, who wouldn't have been here without Damian and Chris.

Our lives moved on, and theirs did as well, changing jobs and moving away from the area, but we stayed in touch via social media. On their birthdays, Christmas and New Year, I'd always send them a message to say thank you and tell them what we'd been up to. To remind them of all the things that they'd made possible for us.

In time, we told each of the children what had happened that day and explained just how brave Chris and Damian had been. We showed them photos and newspaper cuttings, and, of course, Rae had her bear. It was always kept in pride of place in her bedroom. We made sure they all knew exactly who the RNLI were and why they were so important. If you asked any of them, they'd all give the same answer.

Because they saved my family.

Truth be told, the day of the incident never left me. I suffered flashbacks and nightmares, and I panicked whenever the kids went any further than ankle-deep into the water. But it also made me see everything my family did as a miracle. First steps, first words, even first tantrums. I took none of it for granted, because I was always aware of how easily none of it might have happened.

Ten years after the rescue the RNLI got in touch. They were launching a campaign about saving lives at sea and wanted us to make a film for *The One Show* about our story.

'Of course,' I agreed immediately. Since the rescue, we'd helped raise awareness whenever we would. Rae had even opened special exhibitions and spoken to journalists about our experience.

She was becoming quite the ambassador.

They took us back to the beach and we walked them through what had happened, showing them where we'd got stuck and talking about how brilliant the RNLI lifeguards had been.

Then, as we neared the front of the lifeguards' unit, I saw two familiar figures. They were a little older, but I recognised them instantly.

'Chris! Damian!' I exclaimed.

'Hi Vicky,' Damian said.

There was a flurry of hugs and handshakes, followed by stunned silence. We'd had no idea what the RNLI had been planning. But it was a perfect moment.

'This is a wonderful surprise,' I said. 'It's so good to see you both.'

'Do you recognise this one?' Marc said, pointing at Rae.

It was the first time since she was a month old that they'd seen Rae in person.

'This can't be Rae!' said Damian.

'It is!' she giggled.

'Do you know the story about what happened on that day?' Chris asked her, as we chatted together.

'I was in Mummy's tummy. They were walking on the beach and the tide cut them off. Then you two came and saved them,' she said.

Chris nodded in agreement.

'That's right,' he said.

Rae paused for a minute, then she spoke.

'Were my mummy and daddy brave?' she asked.

My heart melted. We all knew who it was that had been brave that day, but it was a sweet thing to ask. Chris looked up at me and Marc, then back to Rae.

'They were very brave,' he said. 'Very, very brave. Your daddy held onto your mummy very tightly and they did everything to keep you safe.'

'OK,' Rae said, smiling. Then she grabbed her special bear from me. We'd been asked to bring it for the film. It was still in its presentation box, but the signatures were fading.

'Will you sign this for me again?' she asked.

'Of course,' Chris said.

When we took it home that evening, it once again took pride of place in her bedroom, where it remains to this day.

The kids are growing up fast now. Rae is ten, and in September she's starting secondary school. Dillon is eight and Tristan is five. They're amazing, loving, caring little people, all so different and special. They light up our world every single day.

I don't think I'll ever feel like I've said or done enough to repay the RNLI, Chris, Damian and that surfer for what they've given to me and Marc. That day in 2009, Marc, Rae and I could have lost our lives, but instead all we lost was a hoodie, our wellies and a bag of bananas. Damian's and Chris's bravery prevented a tragedy. They're the reason I have my family and I will be in awe of their bravery forever.

ACKNOWLEDGEMENTS

This book would not have been possible without the dedication, skill and kind co-operation of the following people: Harrison Bates, Katie Beney, Luke Blissett, Mark Bolland, Lucy Brown, Hannah Butterworth, Amy Caldwell, Mike Carhart-Harris, Anthony Chambers, Maryna Chambers, Alan Cracknell, Mark Criddle, Adrian Don, Eleanor Driscoll, Hattie Evans, Nikki Girvan, Lydia Good, Sophie Grant-Crookston, Dan Guy, Sarah Hammond, Darren Harcus, Dean Hegarty, Clare Hopps, Roger Jackson, Aileen Jones, Chris Lowry, Gemma McDonald, David MacLellan, Martin Macnamara, Nigel Millard, Marc Murphy, Pete Murphy, Vicky Murphy, Michael Nugent, Sheila O'Driscoll, Damian Prisk, Joanna Quinn, Julie Rainey, Dave Riley, Danielle Rush, Mark Sawyer, Kevin Smith, Rory Stamp, Niamh Stephenson, Paul Stevens, Abi Tatton, Mark Taylor-Gregg, Nathan Williams, Oliver Wrynne-Simpson and Caroline Young.

PHOTOGRAPHIC ACKNOWLEDGEMENTS

Page 1, top: RNLI/Nigel Millard
Page 1, middle: RNLI/Torbay
Page 1, bottom: RNLI/Chris Slack
Page 2, top left/top right: RNLI/Nigel Millard
Page 2, bottom: RNLI/Harrison Bates
Page 3, top left: RNLI/Lerwick
Page 3, top right: RNLI/Nigel Millard
Page 3, bottom left: RNLI/Nathan Williams
Page 3, bottom right: RNLI/Jon Stokes
Page 4, top: Bernard Riley
Page 4, bottom: RNLI/Carl Wilson
Page 5, top: RNLI/Nigel Millard
Page 5, bottom: RNLI/Nathan Williams
Page 6, top: RNLI/Nigel Millard
Page 6, bottom left: RNLI/Ben Gilbert
Page 6, bottom right: RNLI
Page 7: RNLI/Nathan Williams
Page 8: RNLI/Nathan Williams

Lifeboats

Get closer to the lifesavers

For videos showing footage and interviews
from the remarkable rescues in this book, visit:
RNLI.org/stormbook

Follow the RNLI on Facebook, Twitter and Instagram
for the charity's latest rescues, updates and fascinating history:
Facebook.com/RNLI | Twitter.com/RNLI | Instagram.com/RNLI

Thank you for powering the charity that saves lives at sea

Photo: RNLI/Nigel Millard